Featuring Thomas the Tank Engine, Bob the Builder,
Pingu, Fireman Sam, Rainbow Magic and more!

Children's Character Cakes

Debbie Brown

Introduction

Famous and popular characters are usually the first choice for birthday cakes as they are so dear to children. With many licensed products on the market it's easy to theme a whole party around the character, making the day extra special.

These types of cakes are usually my favourite to make – to see a child's face light up when they see their favourite character in cake and sugar made especially for them is worth all the effort put into making it, and of course the day is extra memorable for everyone.

The cakes designed in this book are replicas of some of the most famous favourite characters of our time. To make sure these designs were as accurate as possible I had to include virtually every little detail, making some quite time consuming to produce. Whilst there are many cake decorators who think nothing of spending hours making a beautiful cake, most people nowadays have busy lives and re-creating each and every detail isn't always viable. So to give readers a choice, I've included a selection of mini cake designs with instructions, each of which can be scaled up to a full-size main birthday cake as a quicker and easier alternative.

The clear step-by-step instructions make all of these designs achievable for everyone. Bear in mind that good quality ingredients (especially a sugarpaste that works well) and an ambient temperature with low humidity to work in (as sugar absorbs moisture) are both extremely important in order to achieve good results.

When embarking on a project, always leave yourself enough time. Remember that modelled items can be made weeks in advance so that last minute baking and decorating is not so daunting.

Have fun, as that's what cake decorating is all about!

Debbie

First published in September 2009 by B. Dutton Publishing Limited, Alfred House, Hones Business Park, Farnham, Surrey, GU9 8BB.

Publisher: Beverley Dutton

Editor: Jenny Stewart

Art Director/Designer: Sarah Richardson

Sub Editor: Jenny Royle

Graphic Designer: Zena Manicom

Publishing Assistant: Louise Pepé

Photography: Alister Thorpe

Printed in Slovenia

ACKNOWLEDGEMENTS

Special thanks to my parents Pam and Ray Herbert and my husband Paul for their love and support as always.

My children Lewis, Laura and Shaun, and also Michael and Rachael for not minding the workroom bursting out into the rest of the house, and for a while having to contend with boxes everywhere.

My dear friend, assistant and travel companion Elaine Herbert, her great humour and easy-going nature make journeys around the world easier to deal with.

Thank you to Aysa Acar, my long-term friend and best cake crumb nibbler.

Through teaching and promoting cake sculpture and modelling I am blessed to have many friends and have been fortunate to meet so many lovely people around the world. Thank you to my friend Lorraine McKay, her humour and encouraging words get me through each busy day. Thank you to Jo Tomlinson, Shenaz Lake-Thomas and Julia Duncan for all their enthusiastic help, support and organisational skills, but mostly their friendship. I'd like to mention three more girls, Claudia Hurt, Mary Carmen and Liz Ramirez, thank you for your generous hearts, great company and my initiation into your Cookie Sheet Club.

Renshaw for supplying Regalice sugarpaste.

Alister Thorpe for beautiful photography.

Jenny Stewart and Sarah Richardson for all their enthusiasm and hard work putting this book together.

DISCLAIMER

This book is dedicated to all who have found and love this wonderful art and have been inspired to take their talent further.

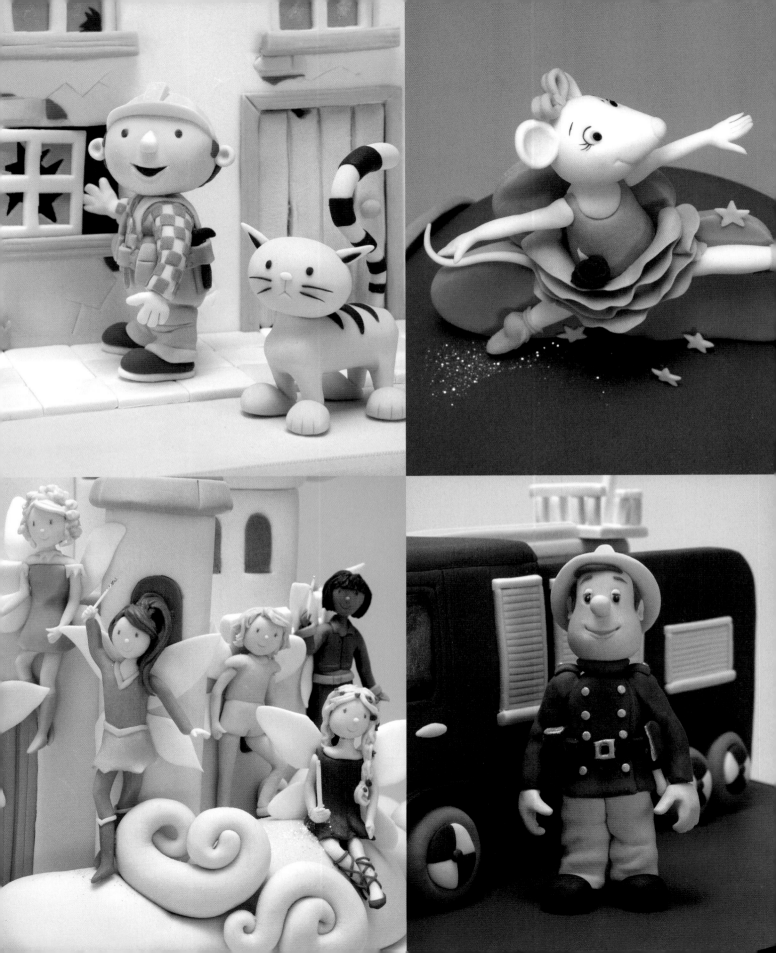

Contents

Recipes

By following the projects in this book you can achieve great results when cake decorating, but of course your cake needs to taste as spectacular as it looks. I've put together a collection of tried and tested cake recipes that are a perfect base for your beautifully decorated cake. All are suitable for sculpture as the texture, although moist, is slightly denser to allow carving and sculpting without crumbling. Always use top quality ingredients to ensure great results.

Unless you're using a professional cake mixture that has additives to ensure moisture is retained, bear in mind that all types of sponge cakes can dry out when exposed to air during cutting and serving. To counteract this, I recommend the use of a sugar syrup just before layering with filling – suggested recipes are given on page 12. This will keep the cake beautifully moist during serving.

If you wish to speed up the baking time of sponge cakes and take the worry out of baking evenly throughout, the quantities given can be split equally between same size tins/pans. This also removes the need to cut layers so saves time.

Top Tip

To settle and limit the crust on the top of the cake and also keep the cake as moist as possible, place a baking sheet over the top of the bakeware whilst baking. When the cake is baked and taken out of the oven, leave the sheet on top of the tin and only remove when the cake has cooled and is ready to turn out.

Butter Sponge Cake

Nothing is quite like a rich and light butter sponge cake and it is versatile enough to complement many different flavours and fillings.

1 Preheat the oven to 150°C/300°F/gas mark 2, then grease and line the bakeware. Sift the flour in a bowl.

2 Soften the butter and place in a food mixer or large mixing bowl with the caster sugar. Beat until the mixture is pale and fluffy.

3 Add the eggs to the mixture one at a time with a spoonful of the flour, beating well after each addition. Add the vanilla essence/flavouring.

4 Using a spatula or large spoon, fold the remaining flour into the mixture.

5 Spoon the mixture into the bakeware. Make a dip in the top of the mixture using the back of a spoon.

6 Bake in the centre of the oven for the recommended time or until a skewer inserted in the centre comes out clean.

7 Leave to cool in the bakeware for five minutes, then turn out onto a wire rack and leave to cool completely. When cold, store in an airtight container or double wrap in cling film for at least eight hours, allowing the texture to settle before use.

	Angelina Ballerina	Barney	Bob the Builder	Fireman Sam	Oswald	Pingu	Rainbow Magic	Thomas
Bakeware	1 x 25cm (10") round 1 x 15cm (6") round	3 x 10cm (4") square 3 x 10cm (4") round	2 x 18cm (7") square	1 x 25cm (10") square	2 x 15cm (6") bowl-shapes or 1 x spherical	1 x 25cm (10") square 1 x 10cm (4") diameter bowl	20cm (8") round	1 x 20cm (8") square
Caster sugar	510g (1lb 2oz)	400g (14oz)	400g (14oz)	400g (14oz)	285g (10oz)	510g (1lb 2oz)	285g (10oz)	285g (10oz)
Unsalted butter, softened	510g (1lb 2oz)	400g (14oz)	400g (14oz)	400g (14oz)	285g (10oz)	510g (1lb 2oz)	285g (10oz)	285g (10oz)
Large eggs	9	7	7	7	5	9	5	5
Self-raising flour	650g (1lb 7oz)	510g (1lb 2oz)	510g (1lb 2oz)	510g (1lb 2oz)	340g (12oz)	650g (1lb 7oz)	340g (12oz)	340g (12oz)
Vanilla essence (extract)	5ml (1tsp)	5ml (1tsp)	5ml (1tsp)	5ml (1tsp)	5-10ml (1-2tsp)	5ml (1tsp)	5-10ml (1-2tsp)	5-10ml (1-2tsp)
Baking time	1¼-1½ hours	1-1¼ hours	1-1¼ hours	1¼-1½ hours	1¼-1½ hours	1¼-1½ hours	1¼-1½ hours	1-1¼ hours

Pink Raspberry Cake

This not only looks pretty, it complements some of the more girly designs in this book perfectly. The addition of raspberry jelly (jell-o) and using egg whites makes the mixture a beautiful pink colour and gives it a great fruity flavour.

1 Preheat the oven to 150°C/300°F/gas mark 2, then grease and line the bakeware.

2 Sift the flour into a bowl. Gently melt the jelly in a pan over a low heat or heat for one minute in a microwave and then stir until dissolved. Set aside to cool slightly.

3 Soften the butter and put in the food mixer or large mixing bowl with the caster sugar. Beat until the mixture is pale and fluffy.

4 Separate the whites from each egg and add to the mixture, one at a time with a spoonful of the flour, beating well after each addition. Add the melted jelly.

5 Using a spatula or large spoon, fold the remaining flour into the mixture.

6 Spoon the mixture into the bakeware and then make a dip in the top of the mixture using the back of a spoon.

7 Bake in the centre of the oven until a skewer inserted in the centre comes out clean.

8 Leave to cool in the bakeware for five minutes and then turn out onto a wire rack and leave to cool completely. When cold, store in an airtight container or double wrap in cling film for at least eight hours, allowing the texture to settle before use.

	Angelina Ballerina	Barney	Bob the Builder	Fireman Sam	Oswald	Pingu	Rainbow Magic	Thomas
Bakeware	1 × 25cm (10") round 1 × 15cm (6") round	3 × 10cm (4") square 3 × 10cm (4") round	2 × 18cm (7") square	1 × 25cm (10") square	2 × 15cm (6") bowl-shapes or 1 × spherical	1 × 25cm (10") square 1 × 10cm (4") diameter bowl	20cm (8") round	1 × 20cm (8") square
Caster sugar	510g (1lb 2oz)	400g (14oz)	400g (14oz)	400g (14oz)	285g (10oz)	510g (1lb 2oz)	285g (10oz)	285g (10oz)
Unsalted butter, softened	510g (1lb 2oz)	400g (14oz)	400g (14oz)	400g (14oz)	285g (10oz)	510g (1lb 2oz)	285g (10oz)	285g (10oz)
Large eggs	9	7	7	7	5	9	5	5
Self-raising flour	650g (1lb 7oz)	510g (1lb 2oz)	510g (1lb 2oz)	510g (1lb 2oz)	340g (12oz)	650g (1lb 7oz)	340g (12oz)	340g (12oz)
Raspberry jelly (jell-o)	370g (13oz)	270g (9½oz)	270g (9½oz)	270g (9½oz)	175g (6oz)	370g (13oz)	175g (6oz)	175g (6oz)
Baking time	1¼-1½ hours	1-1¼ hours	1-1¼ hours	1¼-1½ hours	1¼-1½ hours	1¼-1½ hours	1¼-1½ hours	1-1¼ hours

Chocolate Swirl Cake

One of my favourite recipes, this cake combines the richness of dark or milk chocolate against the light butter sponge cake, making a great combination. Take care not to mix too much to gain a lovely swirl effect.

Method

1 Break the chocolate into a bowl and place over a saucepan filled with hot water (or in a bain-marie). Stir until melted. Allow to cool until slightly warm.

2 Put the softened butter into a mixer along with the caster sugar and beat at high speed until light and fluffy. Add the eggs one at a time along with a spoonful of the flour and beat well. Add the vanilla essence. Carefully fold in the remaining flour. Fold in the cooled chocolate, taking care not to mix.

3 Bake in a preheated oven at 150°C/300°F/gas mark 2.

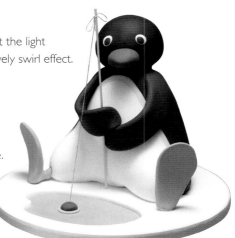

	Angelina Ballerina	Barney	Bob the Builder	Fireman Sam	Oswald	Pingu	Rainbow Magic	Thomas
Bakeware	1 × 25cm (10") round 1 × 15cm (6") round	3 × 10cm (4") square 3 × 10cm (4") round	2 × 18cm (7") square	1 × 25cm (10") square	2 × 15cm (6") bowl-shapes or 1 × spherical	1 × 25cm (10") square 1 × 10cm (4") diameter bowl	20cm (8") round	1 × 20cm (8") square
Caster sugar	510g (1lb 2oz)	400g (14oz)	400g (14oz)	400g (14oz)	285g (10oz)	510g (1lb 2oz)	285g (10oz)	285g (10oz)
Unsalted butter, softened	510g (1lb 2oz)	400g (14oz)	400g (14oz)	400g (14oz)	285g (10oz)	510g (1lb 2oz)	285g (10oz)	285g (10oz)
Large eggs	9	7	7	7	5	9	5	5
Self-raising flour	650g (1lb 7oz)	510g (1lb 2oz)	510g (1lb 2oz)	510g (1lb 2oz)	340g (12oz)	650g (1lb 7oz)	340g (12oz)	340g (12oz)
Vanilla essence (extract)	5ml (1tsp)	5ml (1tsp)	5ml (1tsp)	5ml (1tsp)	5-10ml (1-2tsp)	5ml (1tsp)	5-10ml (1-2tsp)	5-10ml (1-2tsp)
Couverture chocolate, melted	225g (8oz)	175g (6oz)	175g (6oz)	175g (6oz)	100g (3½oz)	225g (8oz)	100g (3½oz)	100g (3½oz)
Baking time	1¼-1½ hours	1-1¼ hours	1-1¼ hours	1¼-1½ hours	1¼-1½ hours	1¼-1½ hours	1¼-1½ hours	1-1¼ hours

Fillings

Sugar Syrup (Moistening Syrup)

Sugar syrup is an easy way to ensure your cake remains moist during the preparation process and, of course, the serving. When preparing your cake, brush or dab sugar syrup carefully over each sponge cake layer, preferably with a silicone pastry brush and before the cake filling is added. The syrup slowly soaks into the sponge until it is distributed evenly throughout the cake. I also brush syrup over the top and sides of the sponge cake just before the crumb coat is spread over the surface as I find it spreads a little easier.

Some cake decorators prefer to be generous when brushing on the syrup whilst others are more conservative – it purely depends on personal choice. I find excessive sugar syrup can cause the sponge to become very sweet, so I recommend the following quantity for a 25cm (10") cake. You can, of course, add more; in fact, many cake decorators use double this quantity.

Ingredients

115g (4oz) caster
(superfine) sugar

125ml (4½fl oz) water

5ml (1tsp) flavouring
(optional)

Method

1 Pour the measured sugar into a saucepan along with the water. Heat gently and bring to the boil, stirring carefully. Do not leave unattended as sugar can burn easily. Simmer for one minute to ensure all the sugar granules have dissolved completely. Remove from the heat and set aside to cool. Store in an airtight container and refrigerate. Use within one month.

2 Flavouring sugar syrup is not absolutely necessary but if you've baked a flavoured sponge cake then flavouring the sugar syrup to complement it can really enhance the taste. Although the most popular flavouring is vanilla, different seedless fruit jams also work very well.

Buttercream

A great versatile filling and the first choice for many, buttercream made with real unsalted butter is delicious. The basic recipe can be flavoured if required to suit your preference.

This recipe makes approximately 625g (1lb 6oz), enough for each of the projects in the book, plus a little extra just in case.

Ingredients

175g (6oz) unsalted butter,
softened

10ml-15ml (2tbsp-3tbsp) milk

5ml (1tsp) flavouring
(optional)

450g (1lb) icing sugar, sifted

Method

1 Place the softened butter, milk and flavouring into a mixer. Mix on medium speed and add the icing sugar a little at a time. Mix until light, fluffy and pale in colour.

2 Store in an airtight container and use within ten days. Bring to room temperature and beat again before use.

Basic variations for buttercream:

Chocolate

Fold in 145g-200g (5oz-7oz) of melted and cooled dark, milk or white chocolate

Orange or lemon

Add 30ml-45ml (2-3 level tbsp) of orange or lemon curd.

Coffee

Add 30ml-45ml (2tbsp-3tbsp) of coffee essence.

Raspberry

Add 30ml-45ml (2-3 level tbsp) of seedless raspberry jam.

Almond

Add 5ml (1tsp) of almond essence.

Ganache

Ganache is a rich chocolate filling and coating, popular with cake decorators as it's not only a delicious filling, but when spread on the surface of the cake as a crumb coat smoothes the surface ready for a neat application of sugarpaste (rolled fondant). Although not absolutely necessary, I recommend you leave the ganache-covered cake to set for 24 hours at room temperature. This allows the surface to set hard, making it easier to achieve great results.

To ensure the ganache sets firm enough to stabilise the cake and make it easier to cover, the cream quantity differs for the dark, milk and white recipes due to the higher fat content of both the milk and white chocolate. Although all three ganache variations will set well, dark ganache will set the hardest. In warmer climates you may need to reduce the cream quantity slightly.

When you're ready to apply the sugarpaste, the ganache covering needs a little sugar syrup, jam or softened ganache stippled over the surface to make it sticky, ready for the covering. Take care not to add too much moisture otherwise your sugarpaste covering may slip.

This amount is enough for each of the projects in the book, plus a little extra just in case.

Ingredients

Dark chocolate ganache

625g (1lb 6oz) dark couverture chocolate

500ml (17½fl oz) fresh single or whipping cream

Milk chocolate ganache

625g (1lb 6oz) milk couverture chocolate

340ml (12fl oz) fresh single or whipping cream

White chocolate ganache

625g (1lb 6oz) milk or white couverture chocolate

170ml (6fl oz) fresh single or whipping cream

Method

1 Melt the chocolate in a bowl over a pan of hot water (or a bain-marie) to 40°C (105°F).

2 Put the cream in a saucepan and bring to a simmer for a minute. Allow to cool slightly.

3 Using a hand whisk, slowly pour the cream over the melted chocolate and whisk gently. Don't be alarmed if the mixture thickens quickly; keep whisking until it is fully combined.

4 Allow the ganache to cool, then transfer into an airtight container and refrigerate. Use within one week.

Icings and Pastes

Sugarpaste (Rolled Fondant)

I have used Renshaw's Regalice sugarpaste throughout this book as it is a good quality brand and is easy to use. Sugarpaste (also known as rolled fondant) is readily available throughout the UK in supermarkets and cake decorating outlets. Each brand has a slightly different texture, taste and working quality, so try different brands to find which suits you best. If you prefer to make your own, I would recommend the recipe below.

Makes 625g (1lb 6oz)

Ingredients

1 egg white made up from dried egg albumen

30ml (2tbsp) liquid glucose

625g (1lb 6oz) icing (confectioner's) sugar

A little white vegetable fat (shortening), if required

A pinch of CMC powder*

* NOTE: CMC is an abbreviation of Carboxy Methyl Cellulose, an edible thickener widely used in the food industry. The CMC you use must be food grade. Brand names include SK CMC, Debbie Brown's Magic Powder (CMC), Tylose, Tylopur, Tylo and Sugarcel. Alternatively, you can use SK Gum Tragacanth, which is a natural product.

Top Tip

To save time when decorating a cake, homemade sugarpaste can be frozen for up to three months. Allow to defrost thoroughly at room temperature before use.

Method

1. Put the egg white and liquid glucose into a bowl, using a warm spoon for the liquid glucose.

2. Sift the icing sugar into the bowl, adding a little at a time and stirring until the mixture thickens.

3. Turn the mixture out onto a work surface dusted liberally with icing sugar and knead the paste until soft, smooth and pliable. If the paste is slightly dry and cracked, fold in a little white vegetable fat and knead again. If the paste is very soft and sticky, add a little more icing sugar. Add a pinch of CMC to strengthen the paste.

4. Transfer the paste immediately into a food-grade polythene bag and store in an airtight container. Keep the paste cool, either at room temperature, or in the refrigerator if the atmosphere is warm. Bring back to room temperature and knead thoroughly before use.

Royal Icing

Royal icing is used to pipe fine details and to stick sugar pieces together as when dry it will hold items firmly in place. Ready-made royal icing can be obtained from supermarkets or in powder form (follow instructions on the packet). If you prefer to make your own, you can follow this recipe.

Makes 75g (2½oz)

Ingredients

5ml (1 level tsp) egg albumen

15ml (3tsp) cooled, boiled water

65g-70g (2¼oz) icing sugar

Method

1. Put the egg albumen into a bowl. Add the water and stir until dissolved.

2. Beat in the icing sugar a little at a time until the icing is firm, glossy and forms peaks if a spoon is pulled out.

3. To stop the icing forming a crust, place a damp cloth over the top of the bowl until you are ready to use it or transfer to an airtight container and refrigerate.

Modelling Paste

This quick and easy recipe makes a high quality modelling paste. If you prefer to use a ready-made paste, SK Mexican Modelling Paste is ready-to-use and gives good results.

Ingredients

450g (1lb) sugarpaste
5ml (1 level tsp) CMC powder

Method

Knead the CMC into the sugarpaste. The sugarpaste will start to thicken as soon as the CMC is incorporated so can be used immediately. The paste will continue to thicken gradually over a period of 24 hours. The amount of CMC can be varied depending on usage and on the room temperature and humidity, so adjust accordingly to achieve the required consistency. Store in an airtight container.

Edible Glue

This recipe makes a strong sugar glue which works extremely well. Alternatively, ready-made sugar glue can be purchased from specialist cake decorating outlets.

Ingredients

1.25ml (¼tsp) CMC powder
30ml (2tbsp) boiled water, cooled until warm

Method

1. Mix the CMC powder with the warm water and leave to stand until the powder has fully dissolved. The glue should be smooth and have a soft dropping consistency. If the glue thickens after a few days, add a few more drops of water.

2. Store in an airtight container in the refrigerator and use within one week.

3. To use, brush a thin coat over the surface of the item you wish to glue, leave for a few moments to become tacky, and then press the item in place.

Sugar Sticks

These are cut or rolled lengths of pastillage, a fast-drying paste that keeps its shape and dries extremely hard. Sugar sticks are used as edible supports, mainly to help hold modelled heads in place. If you are short of time, you can use strands of dried, raw spaghetti. Whichever option you choose, remember to remove the supports before the figures are eaten.

Makes around 10-20 sugar sticks

Ingredients

5ml (1 level tsp) royal icing, made to stiff peak consistency
1.25ml (¼tsp) CMC powder
icing sugar in sugar shaker

Method

1. Knead the CMC into the royal icing until the mixture thickens and forms a paste. If the paste is slightly wet, knead in a little icing sugar until the paste is soft and pliable.

2. Either roll out the paste and cut into different sized strips of various lengths using a plain-bladed knife, or roll individual sausages of paste to the sizes required. Leave to dry, preferably overnight on a sheet of food-grade foam sponge. When completely dry, store in an airtight container.

Basic Equipment

There is a wide variety of equipment available today to help you achieve brilliant results with your cake designs. If you already have sugarcraft tools or you have a good local supplier, please feel free to make the most of the items you have. I am well known for not using much equipment, and I always bear in mind that there may be readers from other countries who may not have the choice that we have here in the UK. I usually only use what is absolutely necessary and specialist equipment that I would highly recommend – items that I use over and over again which are favourites in my small workbox.

Each project gives a comprehensive list of what you will require to decorate the cake, but the items here will give you the basics to get started. A list of recommended suppliers starts on page 94.

Bakeware

Cake tins are available to buy or hire from sugarcraft shops in a huge range of shapes and sizes. For smaller cakes, choose from oven-safe bowls, flexible silicone bakeware and mini cake pans, depending on the project you are making.

Turntable

A turntable allows you to work on the sides of a cake without having to handle it. Make sure the turntable you choose has a good height, i.e. elevates your work to a level that you are comfortable with. Metal turntables are the most sturdy but well-made plastic ones are the most readily available. All turntables can hold a good weight but make sure the one you use keeps the cake level without rocking from side to side.

Rolling pins

Large and small polypropylene rolling pins are a good investment as they are durable and will last for years if looked after well. Use a large one for rolling out cake coverings and a small one for smaller decorations.

Cake smoother

This will help to create a smooth, professional finish when covering cakes and boards with sugarpaste.

Small, plain-bladed knife

You will need a small knife to cut and trim ready-to-roll pastes (such as sugarpaste and modelling paste). Make sure the handle doesn't impede your movement when cutting.

Dowelling rods

These are invaluable as supports for large cakes and can also be used as internal supports for large modelled items. I always use plastic rather than wooden dowels.

Sugar shaker

This isn't an absolute necessity as icing sugar could easily be sprinkled by hand, but it is very useful when rolling out paste. Choose a shaker with generous holes in the lid.

Paintbrushes

I always use good quality artists' paintbrushes as these hold paint and sugar glue well and the hairs do not mark the surface of sugarpaste. I also use brushes to pick up small items so as not to squash them. A range of sizes is available from your local sugarcraft shop – use the round brushes for painting and the flat brushes for dusting.

Cake drums and boards

15mm thick cake drums, often referred to as cake boards, are food safe and lightweight but still strong enough to hold the weight of a heavy cake. The thinner boards (5mm) are still strong and can be used as an alternative to cake drums if preferred.

Cake cards

I use cake cards as separators for tall cakes such as Bob the Builder's house. As an alternative (particularly in America), you may find that food-grade foam boards or plastic plates are more readily available. As long as the separator is safe to use with food it does not matter which you choose.

Cutters

There are many different cutters available – I tend to use basic flower shapes (blossoms, rose petals and daisies) and simple shapes (such as circles, hearts and squares). Plunger cutters are ideal for tiny shapes.

Other useful equipment:

Ball tool or bone tool
Cake leveller/layer cutter
Cocktail sticks
Craft knife
Fine scissors
Food-grade foam sponge
Non-stick board
Non-toxic glue stick
Palette knives (straight and cranked)
Pastry brush
Piping bags
Piping nozzles (various sizes)
Ribbon
Ruler
Serrated carving knife
Small pots or paint palette for colour mixing

Basic Techniques

All of the projects in this book require the cake to be layered, filled and crumb-coated with your chosen filling (see pages 12 to 13). Following these basic instructions will give you a level surface on which to work, allowing you to achieve the best possible results when the cake is decorated.

I have also given guidelines for a few other basic cake decorating techniques to help you achieve great results.

Preparing a Sponge Cake

1 Trim the crust from the cake and level the top with a cake leveller. Cut two to four layers in the cake and brush each layer with sugar syrup to keep it moist (see page 12). Sandwich the layers together with cake filling, up to 0.5cm (just under ¼") deep.

2 Brush more sugar syrup over the surface of the cake before applying the crumb coat.

3 Using a large palette knife, spread an even layer of cake filling over the surface of the cake. Spread evenly to fill any gaps and create a smooth surface. If crumbs start to appear, add a little more filling and skim over the top surface.

4 Leave the cake to firm or refrigerate until you are ready to cover it with sugarpaste. Prior to covering, rework the crumb coat with the palette knife to make it soft enough for the sugarpaste to stick, or brush a little sugar syrup over the surface.

Covering a Cake with Sugarpaste

All-in-one method (suitable for most cakes):

1 Knead the required amount of sugarpaste on a non-stick board dusted with icing sugar. Keep rotating the paste to create an even shape and ensure that it doesn't stick to the board. Do not turn the paste over as the icing sugar underneath may mark the surface.

2 Use a large rolling pin to roughly measure the cake covering area (i.e. across the top and down the sides) and roll out the paste to the required size with a thickness of 3mm-4mm ($^1/_8$").

3 Lightly sprinkle the top of the sugarpaste with icing sugar to prevent sticking. To lift the paste, gently place the rolling pin in the centre and lightly fold the paste back over the rolling pin. This will prevent the paste from stretching and tearing. Lift carefully and position over the cake.

4 Smooth the covering down and around the cake with the palm of your hand, pressing gently around the sides to remove any air bubbles.

5 When you have smoothed over the top and sides of the cake, trim away the excess paste from around the base of the cake using a plain-bladed knife. Rub the surface gently with a cake smoother to remove any imperfections and achieve a smooth surface. After smoothing the sides, you may need to re-trim around the base once again to create a neat edge.

6 If you need to work on the sugarpaste while it is still soft, do this straight away. Otherwise, leave the sugarpaste for several hours as this will give you a firm surface on which to work.

> ## Top Tip
> Occasionally, especially when covering unusual cake shapes such as Oswald, you may find you have a stubborn pleat in the sugarpaste. It is often quicker to pinch it together and cut away the spare paste than to stretch it out and smooth it over. To remove the cut line, press the join closed by pinching gently and then rub with your hands until the join is blended in. A little icing sugar on your fingers will help to remove the line completely.

Top and sides separately (suitable for cakes where sharp edges are required such as Thomas):

1 Roll out the sugarpaste as described in step 1 of the all-in-one method. This time, instead of rolling out the sugarpaste

big enough to cover the whole cake, roll out a piece only the size of the area you wish to cover. Cut a neat shape, using a template if necessary or measure carefully with a ruler.

2 Using a palette knife, carefully lift the paste to avoid tearing or distorting the shape and apply to the cake. Trim to size if necessary and smooth any joins closed with your fingertips. If you are making a very long piece (e.g. to go all the way around the sides of a cake), lightly dust the surface with icing sugar, roll up the paste and position the end against the cake before unrolling around the sides.

3 Allow to firm for several hours, as above.

> ## Top Tip
> As soon as you take sugarpaste out of its airtight packaging it will start to dry, so always knead it thoroughly and then roll out or shape it as quickly as possible. Re-seal any trimmings in a food-grade polythene bag and keep any spare paste wrapped tightly and stored in an airtight container.

Covering a Cake Board (Drum)

1 Moisten the surface of the cake board slightly with a little cooled, boiled water using a pastry brush.

2 Knead the sugarpaste and roll out on a non-stick board dusted with icing sugar. Make sure the paste is big enough to cover the board and is no more than 2mm-3mm (just under 1/8") thick. When rolling out, move the paste around to prevent sticking but do not turn it over.

3 Carefully fold the sugarpaste over the rolling pin, lift the sugarpaste and position it on the cake board. Gently smooth over the top of the covered cake board with a cake smoother.

4 Hold the board underneath with one hand and, using a plain-bladed knife, trim away the excess sugarpaste from around the edge.

5 To finish the board, you will need to trim the edge with co-ordinating 15mm-width ribbon (this is slightly deeper than the cake board to allow for the depth of the sugarpaste covering). Measure the length needed to go around the board and allow an extra 2cm (¾") or so to overlap at the back.

6 Rub a non-toxic, solid glue stick around the cake board edge, taking care not to touch the sugarpaste covering. Starting at the back of the cake, stick the ribbon around the cake board edge, running your finger along the bottom to keep the ribbon straight. Overlap the ribbon slightly and cut off the excess at the join. Ensure the join is positioned at the back of the cake. **Always trim the board with ribbon after you have finished all the decoration of the cake.**

Dowelling a Cake

If a cake has two or more tiers or is particularly tall, you will need to dowel the lower tiers after they have been coated to make sure that the cakes stack evenly and are well-supported and balanced. To dowel a cake:

1 Make a template of the cake top from greaseproof paper and fold in half twice to find the centre. Draw a circle on the paper around the central point – the circle must fit within the size and shape of the tier that will be placed on top in order to support it. Mark the dowel points evenly around the circle – the number of dowels you need will depend on the size of the cake and number of tiers.

2 Using the template and a scriber (or the tip of a knife), mark the position of the dowels on the cake. Insert the plastic dowels into the cake, ensuring that they are vertical and go all the way down to the cake board. Using a pencil, mark each dowel just above the level of the sugarpaste covering, making sure the pencil does not touch the sugarpaste itself.

3 Remove the dowels, place them on a work surface and line up the bottom of each. The markings may vary, so find the mark that is in the middle and score all the dowels at this point with a craft knife (this ensures the cake stands upright, has no gaps and does not lean). Snap each dowel to size and then insert them back into the holes in the cake; they should each sit level with the cake top.

Important Note

Make sure the dowels and any other inedible items on the cake are removed before serving.

Covering Mini Cakes

Mini cakes are popular at any celebration, either alongside a larger cake or instead of one – and look extremely pretty and stylish when presented well. Suggested designs are given alongside each project which co-ordinate with the style of the main cake, so you can use this as inspiration or create your own designs.

Mini cakes

Mini cakes can be made in several different shapes, including square and round. Although you can cut these from sheet cakes using good quality, deep cutters, I recommend the mini cake bakeware and liners by Squires Kitchen, available from sugarcraft stockists (see pages 94 to 95). These cake pans are purpose-made which makes the job easier, eliminates wastage and guarantees the correct shape and size, no matter how many cakes are required. Silicone bakeware is useful for unusual shapes such as spheres and domes as the cakes can be turned out easily.

To cover mini cakes:

1 If required, cut one or two layers in the cake, depending on the size and shape. For ball shapes (such as the Oswald mini cakes), sandwich the two halves together. Layer and crumb-coat the cake with filling (see recipes on pages 12 to 13).

2 Roll the sugarpaste a little thinner than you would for a large cake, around 2mm-3mm (under $^1/_8$") deep, then cover in the usual way (see pages 18 to 19). Use a cake smoother to press the top and sides smooth.

3 Trim the paste neatly around the base of the cake. You can speed this up by using a hollow cutter the same shape and slightly larger than the mini cake to cut around the base cleanly and neatly. Simply move the cutter down over the mini cake, press it into the excess paste around the base and then remove.

4 Place each mini cake on a small cake card to protect and seal the cake and then decorate as required.

Top Tip

Mini cakes make a great party bag filler as an alternative to the traditional slice of cake. Decorate as required, then place in small boxes or cellophane bags tied with co-ordinating ribbon.

Using Colour

Food colourings are available as liquids, paints, pastes and dusts (also known as powders). Liquid colours and paints are generally used for painting onto sugar; pastes are ideal for colouring roll-out icings (such as sugarpaste and modelling paste) and royal icing; and dusts can be brushed onto the surface of sugar pieces or mixed with clear alcohol to make a quick-drying paint.

Squires Kitchen makes a huge range of colours for cake and food decoration. All of their colours are edible, light-fast, tartrazine-free and glycerine-free and are readily available from Squires Kitchen (see page 94) or your local stockist. If you are not using ready-coloured pastes and icings, you will need to colour them at least two hours before starting a project to allow the colour to develop.

Top Tip

Paste food colours are concentrated, so only add a tiny amount of paste food colour at a time using a cocktail stick until the desired colour is achieved. Blend the colour into the paste by kneading well and allow to 'rest' in an airtight food-grade polythene bag for a couple of hours before use.

Oswald the blue octopus is a gentle, cheerful fellow who is full of curiosity about the world. Here he is with some of his many friends, making this a very colourful cake for small children. If you're short of time, Oswald on his own would still make an extremely fun and appealing cake.

Materials

2 × 15cm (6") bowl-shaped cakes

450g (1lb) cake filling/crumb coat

Icing (powdered) sugar in a sugar shaker

Sugarpaste (rolled fondant): 900g (2lb) blue; 450g (1lb) green

Modelling paste: 115g (4oz) black; 15g (½oz) blue; 35g (1¼oz) green; 5g (just under ¼oz) lilac; 45g (1½oz) orange; pea-sized amount of pale blue; pea-sized amount of pale pink; 10g (¼oz) purple; 15g (½oz) red; 410g (14¼oz) white; 35g (1¼oz) yellow

Edible glue (SK)

3 sugar sticks (see page 15) or dry spaghetti

Equipment

30cm (12") round cake board (drum)

Serrated carving knife

Small, plain-bladed knife

Palette knife

Large and small rolling pins

Cake smoother

Paintbrush: medium (SK)

Template (see page 90)

A few cocktail sticks

1cm, 2cm and 3cm (½", ¾" and 1¼") circle cutters

Kitchen paper or food-grade foam sponge

Ribbon: pale blue

METHOD

Cake Board

1 Knead the green sugarpaste until soft and pliable. Roll out on a sprinkling of icing sugar and place it onto the cake board. Smooth the surface in a circular motion using a cake smoother. Cut off the excess paste from around the board edge using a knife and then set the board aside to dry. Further instructions for covering a cake board can be seen on page 20.

Cake

2 Trim the crust from each cake and level the top. Cut a layer in each cake no more than 2.5cm (1") from the top, so when the cake is assembled into a spherical shape all layers are quite central; this will help stabilise the cake. Fill each layer with cake filling and then spread a layer over the surface of the cake as a crumb coat. Allow the covering to firm.

Oswald

3 Roll out the blue sugarpaste and cover the cake all-in-one, smoothing around the shape, stretching out

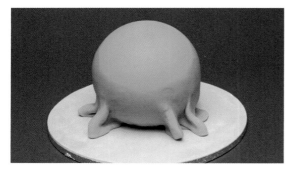

any pleats and smoothing downwards. Some of the excess pleats can be pinched together to form eight tentacles, four on each side. Pinch out as many of this number as you can, trimming away any excess in between each one and smoothing and tucking the edge of the paste underneath for a rounded shape.

4 If you need to make separate tentacles, roll 15g (½oz) of blue trimmings for each one into a teardrop shape, flatten the full end and then stick in position around the base with edible glue. Smooth the join closed with your fingers. Indent his wide smile measuring 10cm (4") from end to end using a paintbrush handle or the lip of a bowl: simply press the lip gently into the sugarpaste surface and tip the bowl upwards. Indent eye sockets just above the corners of his mouth by pressing in with your fingertip.

5 To make Oswald's hat brim, first split 15g (½oz) of black modelling paste in half. Roll one half into a ball and press down to flatten into a circle. To complete the hat, split the second piece in two, making one piece slightly larger than the other. Roll the larger piece into a ball and press down around the sides to flatten the bottom only, making the top of his hat. Use edible glue to assemble the hat and stick it in position. Split the remaining piece of black paste in half, roll into ball shapes and stick in position for his eyes, flattening each one slightly before securing in place.

Madame Butterfly and Catrina Caterpillar

6 Make the two wings first using 20g (¾oz) of orange modelling paste. Roll out to a thickness of 2mm (less than ⅛") and cut out two wing shapes using the template. Smooth around the outside edge of each to soften. Decorate with flattened circles of red, pink and yellow for the spots, each colour graduating in size, and then set aside to dry.

7 To make the butterfly body, split the purple modelling paste into four pieces, two slightly smaller than the others. Roll into ball shapes and then stick together, using the smaller ball shapes in the centre and curving gently upwards at the head. Make the cateroillar using the lilac modelling paste as before, but roll nine ball shapes graduating in size with the largest at the head end.

8 Indent their smiles by pushing the miniature circle cutter into the surface at an upward angle. Make two holes in the top of the butterfly's head using a cocktail stick. Roll tiny round eyes, stick in position and then lay each body down on its side to dry. To make the two antennae, roll a tiny sausage of black paste for each, round off the end and set aside.

Johnny Snowman

9 Johnny Snowman is built up against the side of Oswald so he is supported by the cake. To make the legs, roll 170g (5¾oz) of white modelling paste into a rounded teardrop shape, press down to flatten slightly and then make a cut halfway up to separate the legs. Smooth this cut at the front and the back to soften the edges and gently pinch out his feet. Moisten the side of Oswald and leave to become tacky before positioning Johnny's legs securely against Oswald's side.

10 Roll a 75g (2½oz) ball for his body and stick this onto the legs and against Oswald's side to help support the figure. Push a sugar stick or piece of dry spaghetti into the top, leaving a little protruding for his head

later. Push another support into the body at an angle in the shoulder area, keeping 5cm (2") protruding from his body to help support his waving arm and hat later. Leave to firm.

11 For his arms, split 20g (¾oz) of white modelling paste in half. Roll one half into a short sausage and narrow at the wrist to round off the end for his hand. Press down on the hand to flatten slightly and then make a cut for his thumb, smoothing and pinching around the shape to soften the cut edge. Push this arm down onto the support and secure in place with a little edible glue. Make the second arm in the same way, cutting the thumb on the opposite side and resting the arm against Oswald's back.

12 To make his head, roll 30g (1oz) of white modelling paste into a ball and indent his smile using the large circle cutter. Using a damp paintbrush, make strokes across his mouth area to open it up into a wide smile. Indent a hole in the centre of his face and two eye sockets using the end of a paintbrush. Stick his head in position and add two tiny black eyes and a long teardrop of orange for his carrot

nose. Model black buttons for his chest: he should have three but there is limited space, so make however many you can fit against his chest.

13 For his hat, roll out some black modelling paste and cut a circle using the largest cutter. Roll 10g (¼oz) into a teardrop shape, press down on the full end to flatten and cut the opposite end straight. Stick this in position on top of the hat brim. Secure this hat in position in Johnny's hands, pushing the internal support into the surface. You may need to support this until dry using some rolled-up kitchen paper or food-grade foam sponge.

Daisy

14 To make Daisy's petals, roll a ball of yellow modelling paste and flatten gently with a rolling pin, keeping a circular shape until the diameter is 8cm (3") and the shape is slightly domed. Indent around the outside edge with a paintbrush handle. To ensure the petals are even, indent opposite

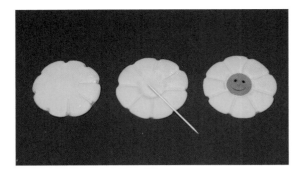

sides first, then mark into quarters and then into eighths. Mark a line from each indent towards the centre and then stroke each at the end so they curve slightly. Press the 3cm (1¼") circle cutter into the centre and then smooth a dip ready for her face.

15 Cut out a circle of orange modelling paste for Daisy's face using the 3cm (1¼") circle cutter and smooth around the outside edge. Indent her smile using the 2cm (¾") circle cutter pushed in at an upwards angle. Indent eye sockets with the end of a paintbrush and then fill with tiny ball shapes of black for the eyes. Model a tiny orange ball for the nose and secure in place. Lay her head flat to dry.

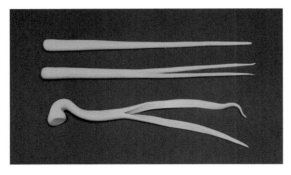

16 For Daisy's body, roll 30g (1oz) of green modelling paste into a long sausage measuring 15cm (6") in length and tapering down to a point at one end. Press on the fuller end to flatten the top. Cut halfway along to separate the legs from the narrow end and stroke down to make them longer and thinner. Stick the body against the back of Oswald, bending the top over into a loop so the flat end is forward, ready to stick against the back of Daisy's head.

17 Moisten Daisy's petals at the bottom of her head and the end of her body with a little edible glue and then stick in place, gently pushing her petals into the surface of Oswald's covering to help support it. For her arms, first put aside a tiny amount of green modelling paste for later and then split the remaining paste and roll into long, tapering sausage shapes. Press each one flat and then stick in position so that they curl round in her pose.

Henry

18 Roll 60g (2oz) of black modelling paste into a teardrop shape, pinch out his tail at the full end and stroke the tip upwards. Roll a 10g (¼oz) teardrop of white modelling paste, press flat and then stick in position onto the front of his body with the narrower end 1cm (¼") from the top.

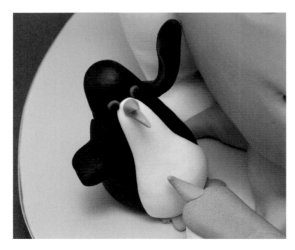

19 For his beak, roll a pea-sized amount of orange modelling paste into a pointed teardrop shape, cut down the centre and then stick the full end onto the top of the white

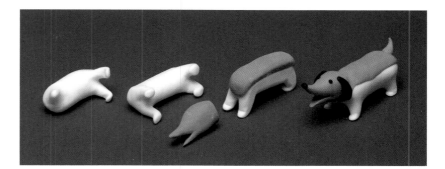

area. Using large pea-sized amounts of orange paste, model flattened teardrop shapes for his feet. Indent into the full end to make them webbed using the end of a paintbrush. Model two blue eyes and stick in position with a slightly smaller black iris. To make his wings, split 5g (just under ¼oz) of black paste in half, roll into teardrop shapes, press flat and then stick in position.

The Egg Twins

20 Roll an oval shape using 35g (1¼oz) of white modelling paste for each body. Indent their smiles exactly halfway up. For the clothing, wrap strips of colour around the lower half of their bodies: cut thin strips of blue and white for one twin and a thicker red strip for the other. Add tiny sleeves and indent at the wrist with the end of a paintbrush to make a hole ready for the hands to slot in.

21 For the legs, use a pea-sized amount of white for each one. To make a leg, roll one piece into a ball and roll one half of the ball into a leg, rounding off the end. Pinch this rounded end forward and shape the foot. Stick in position as each is made.

22 For each hat, model a teardrop shape of red modelling paste and press down on either end to flatten. Stick in position and add a tiny ribbon made from green modelling paste. For the blue hat, flatten a small ball in the centre so the edges tip up and stick in position with a tiny teardrop in the centre. Cut out a tiny pale blue bow tie and secure in place with a little edible glue.

23 For their hands, split pea-sized amounts of white modelling paste in half for each egg. Model into teardrop shapes, press slightly flat and cut the thumb on one side. Slot the point of the teardrop into the end of a sleeve and repeat on the opposite side. Add black balls for the eyes and flatten each one a little when pressing in place.

Weenie

24 Roll the remaining white modelling into a fat sausage and gently pinch four legs, bending the ends forward for paws. Using 5g (just under ¼oz) of orange modelling paste, roll out unevenly around the edge until long enough to cover the length of his body and

down his chest area. Stick in position and smooth around the outside edge. Push the last sugar stick or piece of dry spaghetti into the neck area, leaving a little protruding ready for his neck. Stick on a tiny teardrop-shaped tail.

25 For his head, roll a teardrop with the remaining orange modelling paste and make a cut slightly off-centre to open his mouth. Stroke his muzzle upwards. Indent the back of his head and pinch out a ridge to fit onto his body. Using a little edible glue stick the head in position and smooth the join closed. Add tiny black eyes, an oval-shaped nose and two long teardrop-shaped ears.

Assembly

26 To finish, use a little edible glue to stick the butterfly's body on top of Oswald's head and stick the wings in position either side, gently pushing them into the surface of Oswald's covering to secure them in place. Stick the baby in place. If necessary, use a little rolled-up kitchen paper for support whilst drying.

27 Trim the board with pale blue ribbon.

Mini Oswald Cakes

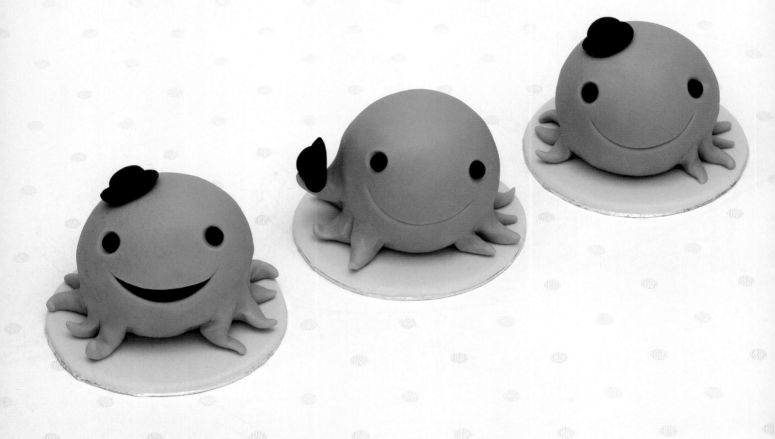

Oswald is such a cute character in himself so I made all the mini cakes the same way, depicting some of the endearing poses and fun facial expressions he has. You'll find that as the cakes are handmade, each expression will come out slightly different, adding to the appeal.

There are many ways to obtain the round shape, especially with the oven-proof and food-safe silicone mould shapes readily available. I used silicone bowls, each 6.5cm (2½") diameter. Alternatively, you can use small cupcake bakeware and trim off the wide top edge of each cupcake. This will make a good enough round shape quickly when covered: as the cake is soft, it is easy to roll the mini cake into a ball as long as the covering is at least 3mm-4mm (⅛") thick.

Materials

6.5cm (2½") bowl-shaped cakes (made using round silicone moulds or small cupcakes with the top edge trimmed)
Cake filling/crumb coat
Icing (powdered) sugar in a sugar shaker
Sugarpaste (rolled fondant): black; blue; green
Edible glue (SK)

Equipment

10cm (4") round cake cards
Rolling pin
Sharp knife
4.5cm (1¾") circle cutter

Basic instructions for covering mini cakes are given on page 21.

METHOD

1 Sandwich the cakes together to make ball shapes and spread a layer of filling over the surface for the crumb coat. Cover each 10cm (4") round cake card with a thin layer of green sugarpaste, or a selection of bright colours if you prefer.

2 To cover the cakes, simply roll out some blue sugarpaste and cover over the whole cake, rolling gently in your hands to make a sphere. Pinch any stubborn pleats to make the tentacles or you can stick these on separately if you prefer. Place each covered cake on a cake card.

3 To indent his smile, push a 4.5cm (1¾") (or similar size) circle cutter into the paste. Follow the instructions for the main cake to make his hat and eyes using 5g (just under ¼oz) of black sugarpaste. You will need a little more black paste to make an open mouth: thinly roll out a little paste, cut a circle and then cut a small slice from the side. Stick in place with edible glue.

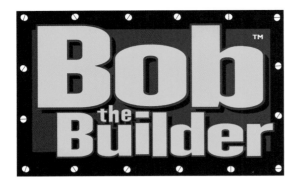

Bob the Builder is an extremely popular choice for a birthday cake as he is so well-loved. Here he is hard at work, as usual, making lots of house repairs with his friend Pilchard the cat looking on.

Materials

2 × 18cm (7") square cakes, each 6cm (2½") depth

450g (1lb) cake filling/crumb coat

Icing (powdered) sugar in a sugar shaker

Sugarpaste (rolled fondant):
   45g (1½") black; 1.14kg (2½lb) cream; 145g (5oz) green; 315g (11oz) peach; 315g (11oz) red

Modelling paste:
   5g (just under ¼oz) black; 45g (1½oz) blue; 15g (½oz) chestnut brown; 10g (¼oz) cream; 30g (1oz) flesh; 60g (2oz) green; 90g (3oz) grey/blue; 10g (¼oz) pale brown; 90g (3oz) pale peach; 30g (1oz) pale yellow; 5g (just under ¼oz) red; 30g (1oz) white; 45g (1½oz) yellow

Edible glue (SK)

3 sugar sticks (see page 15) or dry spaghetti

Dust food colours: black, pink (SK)

Edible metallic paint: silver (SK)

Equipment

30cm (12") square cake board (drum)

15cm × 9cm (6" × 3½") oblong cake card

Serrated carving knife

Small, plain-bladed knife

Palette knife

Large and small rolling pins

Cake smoother

4 food-grade plastic dowelling rods

Paintbrushes: medium, flat (for dusting) (SK)

A few cocktail sticks

Ruler

Templates (see page 90)

1cm, 2.5cm and 4cm (½",1" and 1½") square cutters

Piping nozzle (tip): no. 1 plain

Ribbon: peach

METHOD

Cake Board

1 Knead the peach sugarpaste until soft and pliable, roll out and cover the cake board (see page 20 for full instructions).

2 For the grass, slice away a curved section of sugarpaste at the back of the board and replace with green sugarpaste. Smooth the surface in a circular motion using a cake smoother. Trim the excess paste from around the board edge using a knife and then set the board aside to dry.

Cake

3 Trim the crust from each cake and level the top. Cut both cakes exactly in half. Stack one half on top of the other ready to cut the roof shape. Slice down either side, taking off the top edge of the second layer. Cut a layer in each cake and then sandwich together with cake filling. Place the roof onto the cake card, securing with a dab of cake filling.

4 Sandwich the second cake together and position towards the back of the cake board. Spread a thin layer of filling over both cakes to seal the surface and help the sugarpaste stick. To ensure the base cake has a sugarpaste covering for serving, roll out some cream sugarpaste and cover the top of the cake on the cake board. You may omit this if you prefer.

5 Push four dowelling rods into the base cake in a square around the central point and mark each one level with the top of the cake. Remove the dowels and cut all four to the size of the middle measurement so that there are no gaps and the cake doesn't lean. (See also Dowelling a Cake on page 20.)

6 Place the top cake in position on the dowels. Fill any gaps at the join with cake filling to give a smooth surface and then leave the cake to firm before covering.

Bushes

7 Make the bushes next to allow for drying time. Roll out the green modelling paste, making it slightly thicker at the bottom. Using the template as a cutting guide, cut out the three pieces that make up the bush, keeping the thicker paste along the bottom edge of each. Smooth along the rounded top edge to lengthen and thin out the paste.

8 Roll out more green modelling paste and cut out different sized grass clumps.

9 Thickly roll out the green trimmings and cut three windowsills measuring 5cm (2") in length. Mark the surface of each to create a wood effect using a knife and then allow to firm before sticking in position with edible glue.

House

10 Roll out 400g (14oz) of cream sugarpaste and cut out two pieces to cover the two opposite ends of the cake first. Trim to size and smooth the surface with a cake smoother. Roll out a further 340g (12oz) and cover the back of the cake up to the bottom of the roof line. Close the join on opposite sides with a little edible glue and rub gently with your fingertip to remove the join completely. (More instructions for covering the top and sides separately are given on page 19.)

11 Cover the front of the cake in the same way as the back and then cut out three windows using the large square cutter. Using a sharp knife, cut out a doorway measuring 4.5cm x 8cm (1¾" x 3"). Thinly roll out the black sugarpaste and cut pieces to fit all the windows and the door. To resemble cracked plaster, mark the surface of the cake covering using a knife, indenting areas ready for the brick effect.

Roof

12
Roll out the red sugarpaste and cut a piece to fit over the top of the cake, but make the width measurement slightly larger to create the eaves. Secure in place with a little edible glue. Smooth the surface with a cake smoother; this may distort the edges, so press the cake smoother or ruler up against each edge and push gently back to regain the shape.

13
Roll out the red trimmings and cut out the top of the chimney using the 4cm (1½") square cutter. Cut out a 2.5cm (1") square from the centre. For the chimney, cut out a 3.5cm (1¾") square from cream sugarpaste and then cut an arch on the underside so the chimney fits neatly on top of the roof. Assemble and stick the chimney in position with edible glue.

Windows

14
To make a window, thinly roll out some white modelling paste, cut four 1cm (½") squares close together and then cut around them using the 4cm (1½") square cutter to make the frame. Make two more windows in the same way.

15
Thinly roll out some grey/blue modelling paste and cut three 4cm (1½") squares. Cut out angled shapes from the square to resemble broken glass. Stick the frames over the top and stick two in position in the upper windows. Brush a little edible silver paint onto each window for a glass effect and then set the remaining window aside.

Door

16
Roll out the pale peach modelling paste and cut a piece slightly smaller than the doorframe. Indent lines using a ruler and then cut holes and a ragged edge with a sharp knife. Mark lines with the knife to texture the surface. Thinly roll out the remaining green paste and cut strips for the doorframe. Chamfer the corners, mark a wood effect as before and stick in place around the edge of the door. Stick the door into the doorway and add a tiny green door handle.

17
To make the exposed brickwork, thinly roll out some chestnut brown modelling paste and the pale peach trimmings and cut out small, oblong bricks. Cut some at angles, following the shapes indented for the plaster cracks. Using a dry, flat paintbrush, dust the door, exposed brickwork and the cake with pink and black dust food colours.

Pavement

18
Using the cream trimmings, pale yellow, pale peach and blue/grey modelling paste, roll out and cut eight or nine squares of each colour using the 2.5cm (1") square cutter. Stick these squares in position along the front of the house for the pavement.

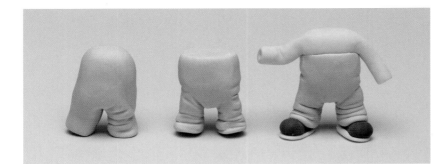

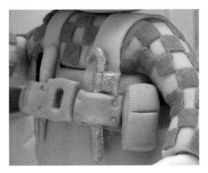

BOB
Boots

19 Roll two large pea-sized amounts of cream modelling paste into short sausage shapes, taper gently at one end and then press flat for the soles. Split 5g (just under ¼oz) of chestnut brown modelling paste in half and roll into fat sausage shapes for the top of each boot. Indent slightly in the centre and back to round off the toe area. Cut away the bottom of each, squeeze the back to narrow slightly and then assemble the boots using a little edible glue.

Bib and Braces

20 To make Bob's bib and braces outfit, roll 35g (1¼oz) of grey/blue modelling paste into a sausage and make a small cut in the bottom to separate the legs. Pinch gently to lengthen slightly and smooth to round off the cut edges. Roll a cocktail stick over the surface to indent folds and wrinkles. Indent the bottom of each trouser leg so they fit neatly on top of the boots. Lay the body down and cut away the

top. Stick the boots in position on the legs and stand the figure up, ensuring it is well balanced and straight.

Shirt

21 For his chequered shirt, roll a 15g (½oz) sausage of yellow modelling paste and make each end thinner for the sleeves. Hollow the end of each sleeve ready for the hands later. Stick the shirt in position on top of the bib and braces and then gently push down the sleeves. Make a slight indent halfway along each sleeve for the elbows and bend into the pose, leaving room for the belt.

22 Thinly roll out a little grey/blue modelling paste and cut two strips for his bib and braces. Stick them in position with edible glue and smooth over the joins. Thinly roll out some red modelling paste and cut into tiny strips and then into tiny squares and then stick these over Bob's shirt for the chequered pattern. Gently push a sugar stick or piece of dry spaghetti down through the body, taking care not to push down too far, and leave a little protruding at the top ready to support his head.

Tool Belt

23 Thinly roll out some pale brown modelling paste for Bob's belt and cut a strip to go around his waist.

24 To make the two screwdrivers, first roll tiny handles using yellow and black modelling paste. Using the grey/blue colour, roll minute sausages tapering to a point, secure to the handles and assemble on the belt with a strip of pale brown covering the join. Indent rivets with a no. 1 plain piping nozzle.

25 To make the wrench, roll a thin sausage of grey/blue modelling paste and form a hook at the top. Stick a tiny strip onto it and indent slightly then stick in position on the belt. Paint with edible silver paint and then cover with a pale brown strip as before.

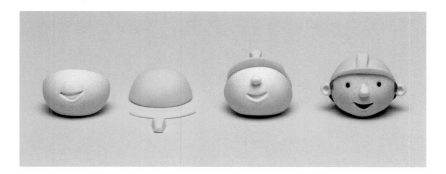

Paint silver on the bottom of each screwdriver. Next to this, make an oblong-shaped pouch and indent lines with a knife. Make another pouch for the opposite side, fold over a tiny strip of pale brown and indent rivets as before.

26 For the buckle, roll out a tiny piece of pale brown modelling paste and push the handle of a paintbrush into the surface, moving it around to make a square hole. Cut around this hole and stick the buckle in position.

27 Cut a small, pale brown oblong for the hammer to rest against and stick in place at the back of Bob's belt. Model a brown hammer handle and then shape the hammer head with a tiny pea-sized piece of black modelling paste, rounding off one end and rolling the opposite end into a downward point. Stick in position with another strip covering the join and indent as before.

Hands

28 Moisten inside each sleeve with a little edible glue and leave to become tacky. To make a hand, roll a large pea-sized piece of

flesh modelling paste into a teardrop shape and press down to flatten slightly. Make a cut on one side for the thumb, cutting down no further than halfway, and then make two slightly shorter cuts to separate the three fingers. Gently push the thumb down and then round off the fingertips. Roll the opposite end into a point to round off the hand and stick the point into the end of the sleeve. Make another hand in the same way, cutting the thumb on the opposite side.

Head and Hat

29 Roll the remaining flesh modelling paste into a ball for the head and then slice off the back from the top, sloping downwards to make a space for his hat. Roll a cocktail stick into the surface of the face to indent his smile, creating a hollow for the black mouth. Stroke just underneath to indent the bottom lip. Press gently on either side and up to his nose to round off his cheeks.

30 Make his hat next by rolling all the remaining yellow modelling paste into a ball and then cutting this exactly in half. Place one half down on the cut side

and stroke gently to widen. Pinch up the paste gently on either side at the top to narrow slightly then stick in position onto his head. To complete the hat, roll the remaining yellow into an oval shape, press down to flatten and thin around the edge with your fingertip. Slice off a long side to make the peak and secure to the hat. Model a tiny wedge for the front and stick in position, resting on the peak.

31 Roll a tiny teardrop-shaped nose and stick in position. Fill his mouth with a tiny piece of black modelling paste and add two oval-shaped eyes. For the ears, split a pea-sized amount of flesh modelling paste in half, roll into ball shapes and then press down into the centre of each using the end of a paintbrush. Stick in position on either side of his head, level with his nose.

Hair

32 Using the remaining chestnut brown modelling paste, model two tiny sideburns and roll the remainder into a tapering sausage for the hair. Press down to flatten and then texture with the paintbrush handle. Stick in position

covering the back of his head up to behind each ear. Brush a little pink dust colour over his cheeks.

Pilchard

33 Roll 20g (¾oz) of blue modelling paste into a fat sausage and pinch out four legs, each one tapering slightly to the bottom. Pinch up a neck at one end and insert a sugar stick, leaving a little protruding ready for the head later. Indent a hole at the opposite end ready for the tail. Lay the body down on its side to firm.

34 Split 5g (just under ¼oz) of blue into four equally sized pieces and model teardrop shapes for the paws. Indent the full end of each leg three times using a knife. Push the end of a paintbrush into the narrower end to make a hole ready for the legs later.

35 To make her head, roll 10g (¼oz) of blue modelling paste into an oval shape and mark the mouth area just below halfway using a knife. Assemble the body and the paws using a little edible glue and then stick the head in position. Add a tiny oval-shaped nose. Make two small, pointed ears and stick them in position so that they are turned down slightly.

36 To make her tail, roll the remaining blue modelling paste into a long, tapering sausage measuring between 7cm and 8cm (2¾" and 3") in length. Push a sugar stick or internal support down into the narrow end and put aside to dry.

37 Using the black modelling paste, roll two tiny oval-shaped eyes, four minute whiskers, two tiny teardrops for the ears and three flattened, tapering sausages for

the markings on her back. To make the stripes on her tail, roll out some black paste as thinly as possible and cut strips. Wrap these around the tail, graduating in size. Take care not to moisten with too much edible glue otherwise the black colouring may transfer and become messy. Gently push the tail into the hole and secure with a little edible glue.

To Finish

38 To finish, assemble the green bush and stick in position on the grass area. Place the window frame into the opening with Bob holding onto it, securing everything with a little edible glue. Trim the board with peach ribbon.

Mini Bob Cakes

These fun designs are quite straightforward to make, although some are a little more time consuming than others. Pilchard is the quickest to make whereas Wendy has more detail so takes a little more time. You could make a mixture of them all, or alternatively a table full of one design would look great. Don't forget that these designs can be scaled up into full size main cakes.

Each face design is baked in the same way using 9cm (3") diameter bowls. You can either use oven-proof toughened glass bowls or oven-proof silicone moulds that are becoming more widely available (see stockists on pages 94 to 95).

Materials

6cm (2½") mini round cakes (made using round mini pans or cut out from a slab cake)

9cm (3") diameter bowl-shaped cakes (made using glass bowls or silicone moulds)

Cake filling/crumb coat

Icing (powdered) sugar in a sugar shaker

Sugarpaste (rolled fondant): blue; chestnut brown; cream; dark blue; dark grey; flesh; pale grey; red; white; yellow

Modelling paste:
    black

Edible glue (SK)

Dust food colour: pink or red (SK)

Equipment

6cm and 9cm (2½" and 3") round cake cards

Rolling pin

Sharp knife

Paintbrush: medium (SK)

Cocktail stick

6cm (2½") circle cutter

Piping nozzle: no. 4 (plain)

Basic instructions for covering mini cakes are given on page 21.

METHOD

Cakes

When the cakes have cooled, layer and fill them if required. To prepare for the covering, spread a thin coat of cake filling over the surface to help the sugarpaste stick and place each cake on a cake card of the same size.

Bob

1 Cover just over half of the cake with a covering of flesh sugarpaste. Trim the excess neatly around the bottom edge and smooth gently to tuck the edge slightly underneath. Indent the smile using a 3.5cm (1½") circle cutter pushed in at an angle. To open the mouth, ease a damp paintbrush into the mouth and gently pull the bottom lip down. To define the bottom lip, stroke underneath using your fingertip. Smooth the paste on either side of face to define the cheeks.

2 Roll out some yellow sugarpaste and cover the top half, trimming neatly as before. Roll a tapering sausage and flatten to make the peak. Model a teardrop for the

front of the hat, press down and cut out the angled shape. Stick both pieces in position using a little edible glue.

3 Model a teardrop-shaped nose and two ball-shaped ears from flesh paste, then indent the centre of each ear with your fingertip. Roll two black ovals for the eyes. Stick all the pieces in position and then add a tiny piece of chestnut brown in front of the ears for his sideburns. Brush a little red or pink dust colour over his cheeks.

Top Tip

Take care when handling the Bob cakes as the ears are quite fragile.

Wendy

Make Wendy in the same way as Bob but use dark blue for her hat, add two red ball-shaped earrings and stick on yellow strips cut to different lengths for her fringe.

Pilchard

1 Before crumb coating the Pilchard cakes, trim slightly on

opposite sides to make her a little more oval-shaped.

2 Roll out some blue sugarpaste and cover her head completely. Trim away the excess paste and smooth the edge underneath slightly. Mark her mouth with a knife and indent four holes for whiskers using a cocktail stick. Make an oval-shaped nose and secure in place with edible glue.

3 Model two pointed ears and stick them in position, pointing slightly downward. Add a tiny teardrop of black paste to each. Roll two black oval-shaped eyes and four tiny sausages for whiskers and secure in place with edible glue.

Top Tip

If you have multiples of this design to make, I recommend using black royal icing and a no.1 plain piping nozzle to pipe the whiskers instead as it is much quicker.

Paint Pots

1 For the mini cake paint pots, use the 6cm (2½") mini round cakes. After you have applied the crumb coat, cover the top of each with a circle of coloured sugarpaste. To cover the sides, roll out some white sugarpaste and cut a strip a little deeper than the height of the cake and 20cm (8") in length. Wrap

this strip around the cake, securing the join closed with a little edible glue. If you have time, stroke around the top lip to thicken it slightly and then indent with a circle cutter (this step could be omitted if you are making multiples of these).

2 To make the paintbrushes, roll 20g (¾oz) of cream sugarpaste into a ball and roll half into a handle. Press down to flatten and then cut the opposite end straight. Cut a hole into the top of the handle using a no. 4 plain piping nozzle and mark a wood effect by indenting lines with a knife.

3 Cut oblong shapes of dark grey the same width as the handles and cut repeatedly into the surface with a knife. Cut some of the brushes at angles along the bottom and then stick in position on the handles. Roll out uneven sausages and teardrops of coloured sugarpaste for the paint spills; these can cover any imperfections in the covering.

4 For the pot handles, roll thin sausages of pale grey sugarpaste and stick in position looped around one side of the pot. Press each end flat and indent rivets with the no. 4 piping nozzle.

There's just something so adorable about Pingu that makes him the world's most popular penguin – his innocent expression and soulful eyes belie his mischievous nature! He appeals to everyone and, as a cake sculpture, would make a stunning centrepiece on the party table and an extra special birthday treat.

Materials

25cm (10") square cake, 6cm (2½") depth

10cm (4") diameter. bowl-shaped cake, 6cm (2½") depth

450g (1lb) cake filling/crumb coat

Icing (powdered) sugar in a sugar shaker

Sugarpaste (rolled fondant): 625g (1lb 6oz) black; 75g (2½oz) blue; 820g (1lb 13oz) white

Modelling paste: 160g (5½oz) black; 125g (4½oz) orange; 10g (¼oz) red; 5g (just under ¼oz) yellow

Edible glue (SK)

Liquid food colour: yellow (SK)

Equipment

35cm (14") round cake board (drum)

Serrated carving knife

Small, plain-bladed knife

Palette knife

Large rolling pin

Template (see page 90)

Cake smoother

Paintbrush: medium (SK)

Cocktail stick

Food-grade dowelling rods: 1 × 23cm (9") plastic and 1 × 28cm (11") wooden

Embroidery thread: silver

Ribbon: silver

METHOD

Cake Board

1 Knead 450g (1lb) of white sugarpaste until soft and pliable. Roll out on a sprinkling of icing sugar and cover the cake board, following the instructions on page 20.

2 Cut out the water area at the front of the cake board using the template. Thinly roll out the blue sugarpaste, cut out the shape using the template and stick it into the uncovered area, smoothing gently around the edge so it fits neatly. Create some ripples in the water with your fingertips and then set the cake board aside to dry.

Cake

3 Trim the crust from the cake and level the top. Cut the cake exactly in half and set one half aside for the base of the cake. Cut the second half into two, so one piece measures 18cm × 12cm (7" × 4¾") and the other 12cm × 8cm (4¾" × 3"). Cut a layer in each cake and then stack them one on top of the other on the base cake, graduating

in size and keeping them central. The total height at this stage should be around 16cm (6¼").

4 Slice down and around the shape, taking off any sharp edges and creating a smooth, rounded surface. The neck area at the top should measure no more than 7cm (2¾") wide. Trim the shape to round off the bottom at the back. To shape the legs, trim at the front to create a ridge where the legs will join the body and then round off the bottom of each. Assemble the layers on the cake board, sandwiching all the layers together with filling and using a little filling underneath to hold it in place. Spread a crumb coat over the surface to seal the surface and help the sugarpaste stick. The total height with cake filling should now be around 18cm (7").

5 For the head, slice the crust away centrally at the top of the small bowl-shaped cake to flatten it slightly, keeping the edge rounded. Cut two layers in the cake and sandwich back together with a little cake filling. Turn over and crumb coat the surface as before. Put both cakes aside for the surfaces to firm before covering.

Pingu

6 Split the orange modelling paste in half. To make a webbed foot, roll one piece into a teardrop shape. Gently pinch and roll out a short leg from the narrow end. Press down onto the opposite end to flatten and then stroke around the edge to thin out. Smooth gently over the whole surface to remove any imperfections. Bend the toe area slightly forwards and then lay the foot down on its side to dry. Repeat to make the second foot.

7 Roll out 450g (1lb) of black sugarpaste and cover Pingu's back, shoulders and sides. Cut a neat edge around the bottom, tuck the edge of the paste under slightly and cut around the sides and chest area, removing any excess paste. Round off the cut edge with your fingertip, creating a lip.

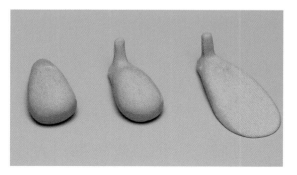

8 Roll out the remaining white sugarpaste and cut an arch at the top that follows the contours of Pingu's white patch. Gently place the covering against Pingu's body, smoothing and stretching the paste into place and stroking it downwards. Trim away the excess paste from around the base and indent and highlight the shape around his legs. Make a small hole in the end of each leg ready for the feet.

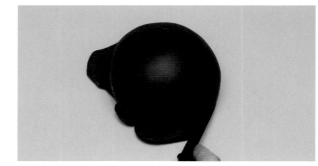

9 Paint a line of yellow liquid food colour around the edge of the white covering at the front, no more than 1cm (¼") wide. Push the smaller dowel down through the body until it touches the base, leaving some protruding to hold the head in place later.

10 To make his wings, first put aside two pea-sized amounts of black modelling paste for later and then split the remainder in half. Moisten the shoulder area on Pingu's body with edible glue and leave to become tacky. To make a wing, roll one piece into a sausage shape measuring 15cm (6") in length. Press down to flatten and lengthen the wing by a further 2cm (¾"). Repeat for the second wing and then stick both in position with one wrapped around the dowel. Push the dowel down into the sugarpaste covering on the board to help secure it further.

11 Re-work the crumb coat to soften it slightly and then roll out the remaining black sugarpaste and cover Pingu's head, smoothing down and around the shape. Trim the excess paste away from the base and then smooth the sugarpaste underneath so that there will be no exposed cake

when the head is in place. Gently push Pingu's head into position, ensuring it is well balanced, and secure at the base with edible glue.

12 To make Pingu's beak, first moisten the area on his face with a little edible glue. Roll 35g (1¼oz) of red modelling paste into an oval shape, place down on the work surface and slice off the back along its length. Stick the beak in position, holding for a few moments until it is secure.

13 For the eyes, model two flattened circles of white sugarpaste and stick them in position with edible glue, neatly spaced and close to the beak. Model two flattened circles of black modelling paste for irises and stick in position, slightly off-centre.

14 To make the float, roll the remaining red

modelling paste into a ball and press down onto the centre to flatten. Secure to the water with a little edible glue. Roll the yellow modelling paste into a sausage and wrap it around the base, securing the join at the back. Moisten the embroidery thread with a little edible glue, make a hole in the top of the red float using a cocktail stick and secure it in place. Tie the opposite end of the thread in a bow at the top of the dowel.

15 Stick Pingu's feet into position and hold for a few moments to secure. If they are a little unstable, use a small piece of white sugarpaste mixed with edible glue to stick them securely onto the cake board. Trim the board with silver ribbon.

Mini Pingu Cakes

All these designs were baked in 6cm (2.5") round mini pans but you could also cut circles from a slab of cake. You could make a mixture of all the different designs, or alternatively a display of one design.

If you'd like one of these designs as a main cake, they can all be scaled up into a full sized cake; Pingu waving from his igloo home works extremely well as a large cake. Follow the instructions here using two deep 20cm (8") round cakes stacked together and rounded off at the top.

Materials

6.5cm (2½") round cakes
(made using round mini
pans or cut out from a slab
cake)
Cake filling/crumb coat
Icing (powdered) sugar in a
sugar shaker
Sugarpaste (rolled fondant):
   orange; pale blue; pale
   yellow; white
Modelling paste:
   black; orange; pale grey;
   red; white
Edible glue (SK)

Equipment

7.5cm (3") round cake cards
Rolling pin
Sharp knife
7cm (2¾") circle cutter
(optional)
Cake smoother
2 five-petal cutters, slightly
different in size
Piping nozzle: no. 4 (plain)
or miniature circle cutter

Basic
instructions for
covering mini cakes
are given on page
21.

METHOD

Cakes

1 Cover the cake cards with
sugarpaste to match the designs:
use white for the igloo and Robby
designs and orange (or your chosen
colour) for the flower cakes.

2 To prepare for the covering,
layer and fill the cakes if
required then spread a crumb
coat over the surface to help the
sugarpaste stick. Place each cake on a
matching cake card.

Igloo

1 You will need a slightly deeper
round mini cake to achieve
the required height for this design,
approximately 7cm (2¾") deep.
Leave the rounded top where the
cake has risen to help shape the
domed top. Roll out some white
sugarpaste and cover the cake
completely, smoothing down and
around the shape. To trim the base,
place a 7cm (2¾") circle cutter
straight over the top and press down
around the base, cutting the edge
cleanly and neatly. Alternatively, trim

neatly with a sharp knife. Position the
cake slightly off-centre on the card,
leaving room for the doorway at the
front.

2 Cut a strip of white sugarpaste
for the doorframe and secure
it in position with edible glue. Roll out
some pale yellow sugarpaste and cut
a door to fit the space. Stick a tiny
oval-shaped door handle onto the
door and then set aside to dry.

3 To ensure that Pingu's head is
held securely against the side
of the cake, cut a small area away
from the frame. Roll a small piece of
black modelling paste and stick into
the doorway for his body. Model a
flattened sausage shape for his wing
and then roll an oval-shaped head.
Stick in position with a little edible glue.
Model his red oval-shaped beak and
stick in position with flattened circles
of white and black to make his eyes.
Stick the door in position slightly ajar.

Pingu and Flower

1 Level the top of the cake to
make it flat then cover with
white sugarpaste. Use a smoother to
smooth the top flat. Cut around the
base as before using a slightly larger

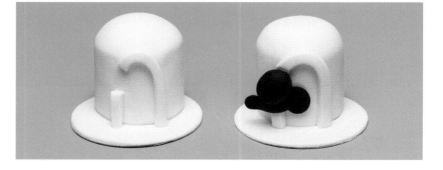

cutter or sharp knife and then place on the covered cake card.

2 To make the flower shapes, I used two five-petal cutters, one slightly smaller than the other. Roll out some modelling paste in the same colour as the base and cut out three large flowers, then cut out the centre of each with the smaller cutter. Leave the shapes to firm slightly before sticking in position with edible glue.

Top Tip

To add a splash of colour to the party table, these look especially pretty in different colour ways if you decide to make more than one.

3 To make the model of Pingu, roll a teardrop shape using 35g (1¼oz) of white modelling paste and gently pinch out two legs at the base on either side. Indent a hole into the bottom of each leg ready for the feet later.

4 Roll out 15g (½oz) of black modelling paste and use this to cover Pingu's back, shoulders and sides, keeping the edge neat. Trim away the excess paste from around the base. Split 5g (just under ¼oz) of black modelling paste in half and roll into sausages, press flat and then stick on either side of his body for his wings.

5 Roll his oval shaped head using 10g (¼oz) of black modelling

paste, model his red oval shaped beak and stick on two flattened white circles for his eyes. The quarter-moon 'smiley' effect eyes are cut from a no. 4 plain piping nozzle or miniature circle cutter.

6 For his feet, split 5g (just under ¼oz) of orange modelling paste in half and follow the main instructions on how to shape. Stick in position with edible glue.

Robby the Seal

1 Robby is Pingu's best friend and makes a cute mini cake with him waving from the ice hole. To make, cover the basic round cake as before but then cut a circle from the top, removing the sugarpaste and filling with a thin circle of pale blue. Stroke ripples into the surface for a water effect using your fingertip.

2 To make Robby, stick a small circle of grey modelling paste onto the centre of the cake top for his body. Make two wings in the same way as for Pingu, turning one up into a wave. For his head, roll 15g (½oz) into a teardrop shape and cut the narrow end to open his mouth. Turn up his top lip by stroking the paste gently upward. Stick in position on the body and then model a little black nose and flattened circles of white and black for his eyes.

Top Tip

If there are any imperfections in the covering, add tiny little water splashes made from blue paste to hide them.

In the Reverend W. Awdry's famous stories, cheeky little Thomas is always trying to be extra friendly and helpful – he wants to be a Really Useful Engine! Thomas was created over 60 years ago and is still a household name, loved by children the world over. Reproduced here as a fun novelty cake, he is sure to make any birthday celebration extra special.

Thomas & Friends © 2009
Gullane (Thomas) Limited.

Materials

20cm (8") square cake 6cm (2½") depth

450g (1lb) cake filling/crumb coat

Icing (powdered) sugar in a sugar shaker

Sugarpaste (rolled fondant):

340g (12oz) black; 770g (1lb 11oz) blue; 340g (12oz) dark grey; 340g (12oz) lime green; 250g (8¾oz) pale grey

Modelling paste:

20g (¾oz) black; 90g (3oz) blue; 115g (4oz) brown; 30g (1oz) dark grey; 60g (2oz) pale grey; 90g (3oz) red; 10g (¼oz) yellow

Edible glue (SK)

Equipment

35cm (14") oval-shaped cake board (drum)

Serrated carving knife

Small, plain-bladed knife

Palette knife

Large and small rolling pins

Cake smoother

Texture mat or new plastic kitchen scourer

Paintbrush: medium (SK)

Ruler

Templates (see page 90)

Small piece of card

3cm (1¼") square cutter

0.5cm, 1cm, 1.5cm, 4.5cm, 5cm, 6cm 7cm and 7.5cm (3") (¼", 3/8", ½", 1¾", 2", 2¼", 2¾" and 3") circle cutters

Piping nozzle (tip): no. 1.5 plain

Ribbon: silver

METHOD

Cake Board

1 Knead the dark grey sugarpaste until soft and pliable. Roll out into a long strip measuring 18cm (7") wide to a thickness of 2mm-3mm (less than 1/8"). Position it down the centre of the cake board. Texture the surface by pressing the texture mat or kitchen scourer repeatedly into the covering. Trim the excess paste from around the board edge using a knife then set aside to dry.

Cake

2 Trim the crust from the cake and level the top. Cut the cake in half and then cut a layer in each half. Place all the layers on top of each other. To shape the coal storage at the back of the engine, cut out a wedge from the back end measuring 3cm (1¼"), cutting down to a depth of 3cm (1¼"). Lay this wedge of cake down flat and cut a curve, rounding off one side ready for the front of the engine at the base. Cover so it doesn't dry out and then set aside for later.

3 Cut a wedge from the top front area of the engine next, cutting down to a depth of 4cm (1½") and leaving an area for the cabin measuring 5cm (2"). This wedge of cake will form the rounded top of the engine. Trim 2cm (¾") from either side of this piece so the rounded part at the top measures between 5cm and 6cm (2" and 2¼") wide and 12cm (4¾") long. Trim to round off.

4 Position the rounded piece on top of the cake. Cut down 3cm (1¼") from the face to shape the sides. Position the 6cm (2¼") circle cutter against the facial area and cut around it as a guide. Take out a little cake underneath and then trim the facial area to round it off a little. Trim the top of the cabin so it slants down slightly on either side.

5 Sandwich the layers together with cake filling and sandwich the piece of cake set aside to the front of the cake with the curve uppermost. Position the cake on the cake board, leaving a little more room at the front. Spread a thin crumb coat over the surface to seal the cake and help the sugarpaste stick. The total height of the engine at the highest point should be 14cm (5½").

6 Thinly roll out 145g (5oz) of black sugarpaste and cut a strip to fit around the base of the cake, measuring 4cm (1½") wide. Secure in position and close the join at the back. Smooth this covering so the top edge is in line with the surface of the cake.

7 Roll out the blue sugarpaste and use this to cover Thomas down to just below the black strip. Cut away the top of the paste at the front then down and around the side tanks and wheel covers. Trim away the excess paste just above the black strip around the base, using a ruler to give a neat, straight edge. Smooth the sugarpaste around Thomas' shape and pinch gently to create sharp edges.

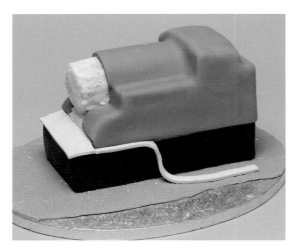

Top Tip

If the paste starts to dry and become cracked or crazed, moisten your fingertips with a tiny amount of cooled, boiled water, dab the area gently to soften the paste and then rub gently to smooth any blemishes away. Take care not to use too much water as this will leave a shine on some pastes whilst others dry with a matt finish.

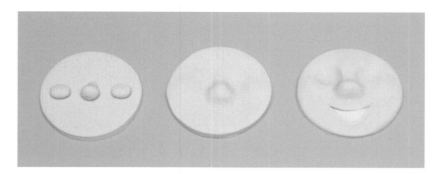

8 Mark three indented lines on either side of the coal bunker using a small piece of folded card cut to 1.5cm (½") long. Cut out the cab opening using the 3cm (1¼") square cutter. Trim a thin oblong window next to it on each side and cut a strip for the door opening. Cut out the portholes using a 1.5m (¾") circle cutter.

9 Put aside 45g (1½oz) of the pale grey modelling paste and then roll out the remainder and cut a strip to cover the top of the front chassis. Cut various strips 1cm (½") wide to fit on either side and around the back of the engine, filling the space between the blue and black paste. Stick in place with a little edible glue.

10 Roll out some red modelling paste, cut four strips and stick in position at the front of the chassis, along both sides and at the back of the engine. Stick two small circles in position to help support the bumpers later. Cut two small squares for the hook and stick in position.

11 Roll out some black sugarpaste and cut a strip to cover the engine around Thomas' face. Cover a small square just underneath,

above the front chassis. Fill the portholes, cab doors and windows with thinly rolled out black sugarpaste. Roll out 45g (1½oz) of black sugarpaste, cut out the cab roof and stick it in place with edible glue. Using 10g (¼oz) of black modelling paste, model Thomas' funnel with two flattened circles on top. Make the two boiler supports for the top and the front chassis, a small hook and model two flattened circles for the buffers.

Face

12 Roll out the remaining pale grey sugarpaste and cut a 7.5cm (3") circle for Thomas' face. Turn the circle over and use pea-sized amounts to pad out the cheeks and make a teardrop-shaped nose. Turn the paste back over and smooth around this padding to bring out the features. Press into the paste gently with your finger to indent eye sockets. Cut his smile with a knife and fill with white modelling paste rolled extremely thinly. Smooth the paste into

the corners with a damp paintbrush. Make two eyes with a little white and black modelling paste and cut out two triangular eyebrows. Smooth gently around the contours of the face and around the underside of his cheeks and bottom lip. Re-cut the face with the circle cutter to remove any excess paste. Smooth gently around the cut edge and then stick in position.

13 To make the track, roll out the brown modelling paste and cut three long strips measuring 14cm × 2cm (5½" × ¾"). Mark lines over the surface of each strip with a knife to create a wood effect. Cut small pieces for the ends of the track and position down either side of the engine, ensuring they are evenly spaced.

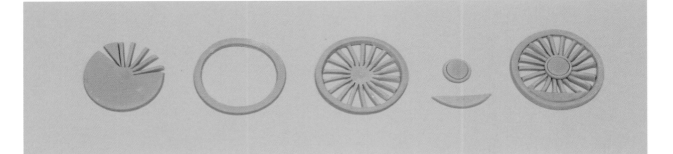

14 Thickly roll out the remaining pale grey modelling paste and cut two long strips for the rails. Leave to firm before sticking in position against either side of the engine and resting on the track. Roll out the dark grey paste and cut tiny squares for either side of each rail. Indent each square with a no.1.5 plain piping nozzle and secure in place.

Wheels

15 To make the six wheels, roll out some blue modelling paste and cut out six hoops using the 4.5cm (1¾") and 5cm (2") circle cutters. Press in the centre of each inner circle with your finger as a cutting guide and then cut out the spokes. Stick the hoops around the spokes with edible glue to make the wheels. Measure the space between the engine and rail carefully and then cut a little from the top of each assembled wheel so they all fit perfectly; however, don't stick in position until dry. Cut out six blue circles using the 1.5cm (½") circle cutter and then indent the centre of each with a 0.5cm (¼") circle cutter. Stick each of these circles in place on the centre of each wheel. Cut a further two 5cm (2") circles and cut six counterweights from around the edge, one for each wheel.

16 When the wheels are dry, carefully stick them in position. Roll out some dark grey modelling paste and cut strips to link them together, indenting into the centre of each by rolling a paintbrush handle over the surface. Cut out six dark grey circles using the 1.5cm (½") circle cutter, another six using the 0.5cm (¼") circle cutter and then stick a small, flattened blue circle onto the centre of each. For the funnel, roll the remaining blue paste into a sausage, cut the bottom straight and then stick in position on top of the engine.

17 Thinly roll out the remaining red modelling paste and cut out all the thin strips for the engine. You may find it easier to allow these strips to firm up slightly before positioning, but don't let them dry completely as they are fragile and will break easily. Cut two number ones using the template. These are filled in later with a smaller cut-out of yellow paste.

18 Thinly roll out a little of the remaining yellow modelling paste and cut strips to edge the door and window. Cut out hoops to edge the portholes using the 1.5cm (½") and 1cm (½") circle cutters. Cut out the yellow centres for the number ones. Model the engine whistles by building up different sized ball and oval shapes.

19 Model all the small angular coal pieces using pea-sized amounts of black sugarpaste and stick them in position at the back of the engine.

20 Thickly and unevenly roll out the lime green sugarpaste, cut in half and use to cover the opposite sides of the board. Smooth gently to create curved lines and trim neatly around the edge.

21 Trim the board with silver ribbon to finish.

Mini Thomas Cakes

These fun face designs of Thomas' friends are quite straightforward to make, and this way children can choose their favourite character. The cakes are baked in round mini pans but only filled up to one third to keep them shallow. As Thomas has many friends, I chose three popular ones to reproduce as mini cakes. If you wish to make Thomas as a mini cake too, follow the instructions to reproduce his face given for the main cake.

This style of cake also looks great at full size and is a quicker and easier alternative to making the whole of Thomas. To make a full-size version, use a 20cm (8") or 25cm (10") round cake as a base.

Materials

6.5cm (2½") shallow round cakes (made using round mini pans or cut out from a slab cake)

Cake filling/crumb coat

Icing (powdered) sugar in a sugar shaker

Sugarpaste (rolled fondant):
   black; blue; lime green; pale grey; red

Modelling paste:
   black; white

Edible glue (SK)

Equipment

7.5cm (3") round cake cards

Rolling pin

Sharp knife

7cm (2¾") circle cutter (optional)

Basic instructions for covering mini cakes are given on page 21.

METHOD

Cakes

1 Cover a cake card for each cake in the colour corresponding to that engine: Edward is blue, James is red and Percy is green.

2 When the cakes have cooled, layer and fill each cake if required. To prepare for the covering, spread a thin coat of filling over the surface to help the sugarpaste stick. Place each cake onto a covered board that depicts their engine colour.

3 To cover each cake, measure the depth of the cake and then cut a strip of black sugarpaste to this width and measuring 20cm (8") in length. Carefully wrap this strip around the sides of the cake, securing the join closed with a little edible glue.

4 Model a funnel from black sugarpaste. Each character has a slightly different funnel so adapt the shape to suit the character. So the funnel stays in position, cut out a small hole from the cake covering, moisten with a little edible glue and allow it to become tacky. Gently push the funnel in place, hold for a few moments and support with a piece of spare paste until dry.

Edward the Blue Engine - No. 2

Edward's face is similar as Thomas' so follow the instructions given in the main cake but make his nose shape flatter and wider with nostrils. Make his eyes as semicircles and tip up slightly at the outer corners to give an almond shape.

James the Red Engine - No. 5

Follow the instructions for Thomas again but without padding the nose. Model the nose separately as an oval shape and then stick in position in the centre of the face with edible glue. Model teardrop-shaped eyebrows and make semi-circular eyes.

Percy the Small Engine - No. 6

Follow the instructions for Thomas again without padding the nose. Model the nose separately as a ball shape and then stick in position with edible glue. Make his mouth smaller and fill with a little black sugarpaste. Make his eyebrows quarter-moon shaped.

Rainbow Magic © 2009 Rainbow Magic Limited. A HIT Entertainment company. Rainbow Magic is a trademark of Rainbow Magic Limited.

Home to King Oberon and Queen Titania of Fairyland, this pink palace is one of the prettiest ever. Complete with the seven Rainbow Fairies, this will be the ideal choice for any little girl.

Materials

20cm (8") round cake, 6cm (2½") depth

400g (14oz) cake filling/crumb coat

Icing (powdered) sugar in a sugar shaker

Sugarpaste (rolled fondant):
    900g (2lb) blue/grey; 450g (1lb) palest blue/grey; 770g (1lb 11oz) pink

Modelling paste:
    30g (1oz) blue; 30g (1oz) darkest pink; 210g (7½oz) dark pink; 30g (1oz) flesh; 30g (1oz) green; 30g (1oz) indigo (dark blue/mauve); tiny piece of lilac; 30g (1oz) orange; 900g (2lb) pink; 30g (1oz) red; tiny piece of pale blue; 5g (just under ¼oz) pale brown; 5g (just under ¼oz) peach; 30g (1oz) violet; 45g (1½oz) white; 30g (1oz) yellow

Edible glue (SK)

7 sugar sticks (see page 15) or dry spaghetti

Liquid food colour: black (SK)

Edible sparkle powder or food-safe glitter (SK)

Royal icing:
    5g (just under ¼oz) each of black; chestnut brown; dark brown; golden yellow; yellow

Equipment

35cm (14") round cake board (drum)

Serrated carving knife

Small, plain-bladed knife

Palette knife

Large and small rolling pins

Cake smoother

Paintbrushes: fine, medium (SK)

Cocktail stick

4 food-grade plastic dowelling rods

Ruler

Sheet of card

Templates (see page 91)

1cm (½") square cutter

4cm (1½") circle cutter

5 piping bags

Piping nozzle (tip): no. 4 plain

Ribbon: pale blue

METHOD

Cake Board

1 Knead the palest blue sugarpaste until soft and pliable and cover the cake board (see page 18 for full instructions). Set the board aside to dry.

Cake

2 Trim the crust from the cake and level the top. Cut layers and sandwich them back together with cake filling (see page 18). Place the cake very slightly off centre towards the right hand side on the cake board and secure in place with a dab of cake filling. Spread a layer of filling over the surface to help the sugarpaste stick. Leave the cakes to firm before covering.

3 Roll out 200g (7oz) of pink sugarpaste and cover the top of the cake only. Trim neatly around the edge and smooth the surface with a cake smoother.

4 To cover the front of the cake, roll out 115g (4oz) of pink sugarpaste and cut an oblong measuring 12cm (5") wide and 14cm (5½") high. Cut out the battlements along the top using the small square cutter. Brush a little edible glue along the cut edge of the cake covering and then press this piece gently into position at the front of the cake. Use a cake smoother to achieve a dimple-free surface.

5 Make the window and door templates from card. Cover the remaining sides of the cake in two sections, leaving a space in between each section to allow for the three turrets and cutting each piece to a total height of 11cm (4½''). Cut the doorway out of the front using the template. Press the large window template into the soft sugarpaste covering to indent three windows on the left-hand side of the castle.

Turrets and Walls

6 Make all the turrets next to allow for drying time using pink modelling paste. To make the three turrets that are positioned around the cake sides, split 400g (14oz) of pink modelling paste into three, roll into sausages measuring 14cm (5½'') in length and cut both ends straight. Press the large window template into the surface of two to indent the paste and then remove. Press the smaller window template into the third turret twice, and then remove. You may need to re-roll each turret if the shape has distorted.

Top Tip

A quick and easy way of rolling a sausage shape and keeping a good shape is to roll it back and forth with a cake smoother.

7 Make the four long, thin turrets next, using 60g (2oz) of pink modelling paste for each. Make two 13cm (5¼'') and the other two 14cm (5½'') in length. Insert a dowel into each turret, leaving around 7cm (2¾'') protruding ready to insert into the cake to help hold them securely in place. Press the small window template into each, re-roll gently to remove any distortion and then set aside to dry.

8 Make the wide, short turret next using 115g (4oz) of pink modelling paste. Roll a short, fat sausage measuring 6cm (2¼'') long and 4cm (1¾'') wide. Indent windows with the small window template and then cut the top and bottom straight as before.

9 Roll out some pink modelling paste to a thickness of 1cm (½'') and cut out a circle using the 4cm (1½'') circle cutter. Pinch around the top edge to widen and then stick in position on top of the large, short turret. Cut a strip and cut out battlements along the top. Stick this around the top edge, leaving a space on one side

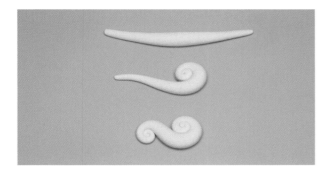

ready for a long, thin turret to be positioned later.

10 Cut out the wall linking the central turrets next, measuring 8cm x 4cm (3¼" x 1½"). Cut out battlements along the top edge. Cut out the small bridge linking the two turrets on the left, measuring 3cm x 4cm (1¼" x 1 ½"). Cut out battlements along the top, bend forward slightly and then put both pieces aside to dry.

11 To make the small turret and wall on the far left, roll 20g (¾oz) of pink modelling paste into a sausage and cut both ends straight to a total length of 8cm (3"). For the wall, thickly roll out more pink paste and cut out the wall shape using the large door template as a guide and then cut it down to a height of 7cm (2¾"). Put both aside to dry.

Rainbow

12 Roll out 10g (¼oz) each of the rainbow colours and cut strips using the rainbow template. Stick them together with a little edible glue starting with the violet, then indigo, blue, green, yellow, orange and red. Set aside to dry.

13 Roll out 30g (1oz) of dark pink modelling paste and cut a small and a large door slightly smaller than the width of each template to allow for the indented lines. Indent the lines down each door using a ruler and mark lines with a knife for a wood grain effect. Stick the smaller door into the left side wall and the large door into the opening at the front of the cake.

14 Stick the wall in position on the left-hand side with the small turret. Stick the three large turrets in place against the cake, holding for a few moments to secure.

Windows

15 Thinly roll out the darkest pink modelling paste and cut all the large and small windows to go around the cake. Secure in place with a little edible glue.

Clouds

16 Shape the clouds using the blue/grey sugarpaste and stick them around the base of the cake with edible glue. For the curly clouds, roll fat sausages tapering at either end and curl these around, either up or down. Save a little blue/grey paste for the clouds that will hold the rainbow in position later.

Roofs

17 To make the pointed roofs, make the three larger roofs first by splitting 90g (3oz) of dark pink modelling paste into three equal pieces. To make a roof, roll one piece into a pointed teardrop shape and press down on the full end to flatten. Smooth around the shape to straighten the sides. Indent horizontal and vertical lines with a knife for a tiled effect. Using the remaining dark pink paste make five more roofs, one small for the smallest turret.

18 Stick all the turrets and assemble the walls in position on top of the cake, starting with the wide, short turret on the right. Take care not to position it too near the edge: there is a little weight

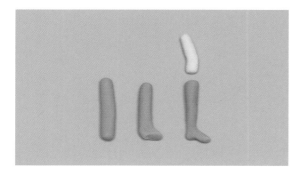

here and if positioned too close to the side it may start to lean. Carefully push each dowelled turret down into the cake and secure in place with a little edible glue. Stick the walls in position, holding for a few moments until secure. Stick the roofs in position.

FAIRIES

Make the fairies next, building them in their poses directly onto the cake. They are made in slightly different ways, depending on what the fairy is wearing.

Legs, Tights and Trousers

19 To make the legs, use pea-sized amounts for each. Roll each piece into a sausage and bend the end for the foot. Pinch to shape the heel and indent to narrow the ankle. Cut the top straight. Pinch up at the knee and push in at the back to shape the leg. For legs with shoes, roll the sausage to taper down to the ankle. For legs with boots, cut off the legs just below the knee.

20 To make trousers, roll 5g (just under ¼oz) of modelling paste into a sausage and cut down the centre to separate the legs. Soften the cut edge by smoothing gently and pinch at the knee to shape. Press the end of each trouser leg flat to widen. For Izzy the Indigo Fairy, stick a tiny oval of pale brown on the top for her midriff.

Shoes, Boots and Socks

21 For shoes, wrap little strips of paste around the leg with the join at the back and smooth gently underneath the foot. Alternatively, roll little teardrop shapes using pea-sized amounts of paste and stick in position. For Fern the Green Fairy, use light brown modelling paste and turn the point upwards slightly. For the Ruby the Red Fairy, add tiny strips of red modelling paste for her laces.

22 To make boots, use pea-sized amounts for each, roll into a sausage and bend around the end for the foot. Pinch to shape the heel and indent to narrow the ankle. Cut the top straight and secure to the legs. Make socks for Heather the Violet Fairy in the same way and add little strips for shoes, as described above.

Wings and Wands

23 Each set of four wings requires 5g (just under ¼oz) of white modelling paste. Split this amount into four pieces, two slightly larger and then model the shapes before pressing down or rolling out.

24 Thinly roll out more white paste and cut tiny strips for the wands, making a few spare to allow for breakages. Allow to dry and then moisten the tip of each with a little edible glue and dip into edible sparkle or glitter.

Dresses and Skirts

25 For Heather the Violet Fairy, roll 5g (¼oz) of violet modelling paste into a fat sausage shape. Mark a line across the top and then mark vertical pleats down the lower half.

26 For Sky the Blue Fairy, make a dress in the same way from blue modelling paste and then pinch around the bottom to hollow out slightly so the dress fits over her legs. Do the same for Ruby

the Red Fairy and pinch some pleats into the skirt. At the top of Ruby's dress, pinch up two sleeves at the shoulders.

27 For Amber the Orange Fairy's skirt, roll out a little peach modelling paste and cut a strip which is slightly scalloped along the bottom edge.

Shorts, Tops and Jackets

28 For the shorts on Saffron the Yellow Fairy, shape a small, flattened square and make a cut at the bottom to separate the legs. Pinch around the bottom of each leg of the shorts to hollow out slightly then glue the legs to the shorts.

29 To make a top, roll 5g (¼oz) of modelling paste into a ball and press down to flatten slightly. Make a cut on either side for the sleeves and gently roll each one down. Indent the end of each sleeve with a cocktail stick to make a hole for the hand later.

30 For Saffron the Yellow Fairy, use a smaller

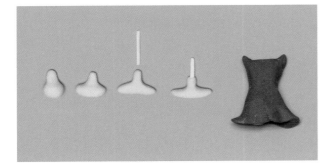

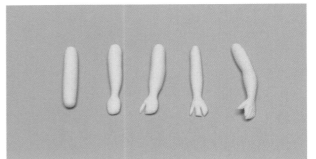

amount for the top and pinch out two capped sleeves at the sides, curving each one downwards.

31 To indent the neck area, either mark a 'v' with the tip of a knife or press down with your finger to indent a curve.

32 For Izzy the Indigo Fairy's jacket, follow the instructions for the top and then cut it short so it will fit neatly onto her body. Mark lines with a knife and buttons with the tip of a cocktail stick. Cut a tiny strip for her collar and use the lilac modelling paste for her cuffs at the end of each sleeve and around the bottom of her trousers.

Necks and Shoulders

Each little fairy has a neck into which a small sugar stick or piece of dry spaghetti is inserted to help hold their heads in position later. However, Fern, Amber and Saffron are supported by the cake so will not need the extra support.

33 To make a neck with shoulders (Sky and Ruby), roll a tiny sausage and roll up a neck in the centre. So this fits neatly onto the dress, cut across the bottom to make a straight edge.

34 For a neck and chest area (Fern, Amber and Izzy), roll a small ball and then pinch up a neck at the top, rolling gently to round off. Push the chest area down into the opening on the body to follow the contours of the clothing.

Hands and Arms

35 To make hands, shape tiny flattened teardrop shapes, cut a thumb from the full end on one side no further than halfway down and make three further cuts along the

top to separate the fingers. Squeeze the fingers together gently and pull the thumb down. Stick the pointed end into the end of a sleeve. As you make each pair of hands, stick a fairy wand into one, stroking the fingers around the bottom to secure.

36 For the arms, roll thin sausages of modelling paste and narrow at the wrist to round off the hand. Press down on the hand to flatten slightly and then cut the thumb and fingers as before. Stick each arm in position with a little edible glue. Some outfits have tiny sleeves to cover the joins which also help to hold them in place.

Heads and Hair

37 To make the heads, roll small oval shapes and press down on the face to flatten slightly. Indent each smile by pushing a piping nozzle into the paste at an upward angle to indent a semi-circle. Add a minute ball for each nose. Using a fine paintbrush and black liquid food colour, paint their tiny 'scribbled' eyes. Carefully push each head onto the sugar stick (if used) and secure to the body with a little edible glue.

38 Prepare the royal icing by placing each colour into a piping bag one at a time. Snip a tiny hole in the tip and pipe all the fairies' hair. Use a damp paintbrush to help move the royal icing around, creating the different hairstyles.

Accessories and Trimmings

39 Model a necklace made up of tiny balls for Heather the Violet Fairy and cut zigzag sleeves and choker for Sky the Blue Fairy. Add a blue belt onto Izzy the Indigo Fairy's trousers. Cut tiny strips of yellow to edge Amber the Orange Fairy's costume. For Ruby the Red Fairy, add tiny dots of red modelling paste over her hair and push into each with a cocktail stick to make flower shapes.

Finishing Touches

40 Stick the rainbow in position supported by two small clouds at the back of the cake and support until dry. Trim the board with pale blue ribbon and sprinkle the cake with edible sparkle dust or edible glitter.

Top Tip

If you're short of time, the castle without the rainbow and fairies makes a stunning birthday cake, or just make one fairy in your favourite colour.

Mini Rainbow Cakes

Materials

6.5cm (2½") round cakes
(made using round mini pans
or cut out from a slab cake)

Cake filling/crumb coat

Icing (powdered) sugar in a
sugar shaker

Sugarpaste (rolled fondant):
blue; green; indigo; orange;
red; violet; white; yellow

Modelling paste:
blue; green; indigo; orange;
red; white; yellow

Liquid food colour: violet
(SK)

Edible glue (SK)

**Basic
instructions for
covering mini cakes
are given on page
21.**

Equipment

7.5cm (3") round cake
cards

Rolling pin

Sharp knife

7cm (2¾") circle cutter
(optional)

Cake smoother

Tiny blossom plunger
cutter

Food-grade foam sponge

Tiny butterfly or heart
cutter

Tiny leaf cutter (optional)

Tiny star cutter

Paintbrush: fine (SK)

METHOD

Cakes

1 Cover as many 7.5cm (3") round cake cards as
required for the mini cakes in sugarpaste coloured to
match the fairy. To make the decoration stand out, lighten
the sugarpaste for the cake and base covering by blending
in some white sugarpaste or by adding slightly less paste
colouring. Ensure you colour enough paste to cover the
cake and base.

2 When the cakes have cooled, layer and fill each cake
if required. To prepare for the covering, spread a thin
coat of filling over the surface to help the sugarpaste stick.

3 To cover each cake, roll out the coloured sugarpaste
and cover the cake completely, smoothing down and
around the shape. To cut around the base, use a slightly
larger circle cutter or trim away the excess paste with a knife.
Use a cake smoother to gain a neat smooth surface and
place each cake on matching sugarpaste covered boards.

4 For the wands, roll small sausage shapes using
modelling paste in slightly deeper colours and set
aside to dry. Stick onto the top of each cake at different
angles with edible glue.

With a matching cake for each Rainbow Fairy, these mini cakes would be extremely popular on the party table or as little gifts for the party guests. I've kept them simple and most of the decorations can be cut quickly with specialist cutters (see stockists on pages 94 to 95).

Ruby the Red Fairy

Thinly roll out some red modelling paste and cut out several tiny blossoms using a small blossom plunger cutter. Push the blossoms out of the cutter and onto into a sheet of food-grade foam sponge to create a cupped shape. Allow to dry before securing to the top and sides of the red cake with edible glue.

Amber the Orange Fairy

Make different-sized orange ball shapes from modelling paste for bubbles and secure to the orange cake with edible glue.

Saffron the Yellow Fairy

A tiny butterfly cutter would be perfect for this design, but these are hard to find. A good alternative is to use a mini heart cutter and then cut out small 'v' shapes from each side to create the wing shape. Indent down the centre of each shape with the back of a knife and pinch them up slightly. Glue to the yellow cake with edible glue.

Fern the Green Fairy

A tiny leaf cutter would be perfect but if you can't find one, model tiny teardrop shapes from green modelling paste. Indent the centre of each leaf with the back of a knife and secure to the cake.

Sky the Blue Fairy

Thinly roll out some blue modelling paste and cut out all the stars using a miniature star cutter. Use edible glue to secure them to the top and sides of the blue cake.

Izzy the Indigo Fairy

Model tiny curled teardrop shapes for the ink drops and secure to the indigo cake.

Heather the Violet Fairy

Use the blossom plunger cutter in the same way as for the red cake and make several flowers from white modelling paste. Paint a little violet liquid food colour into the centre of each flower, allow to dry then secure in place with edible glue.

Barney the dinosaur is a lovable, huggable T-Rex who is adored by pre-schoolers all over the globe. Here he is with fun, giant birthday parcels with delicious cake inside...or perhaps that's where his friends are hiding!

Materials

3 x 10cm (4") square cakes, 6cm (2½") depth

3 x 10cm (4") round cakes, 6cm (2½") depth

595g (1lb 5oz) cake filling/crumb coat

Icing (powdered) sugar in a sugar shaker

Sugarpaste (rolled fondant):
340g (12oz) orange; 450g (1lb) pale blue; 315g (11oz) pink; 315g (11oz) purple; 625g (1lb 6oz) yellow

Modelling paste:
5g (just under ¼oz) black; 60g (2oz) blue; 90g (3oz) green; 400g (14oz) purple; 5g (just under ¼oz) white; 45g (1½oz) yellow

Edible glue (SK)

Equipment

35cm (14") round cake board (drum)

Serrated carving knife

Small, plain-bladed knife

Palette knife

Large rolling pin

Cake smoother

Paintbrush: medium (SK)

15cm (6") food-grade plastic dowelling rod or lolly stick

A few cocktail sticks

Ruler

Bone or ball tool

2cm and 4cm (¾" and 1½") circle cutters

2cm (¾") square cutter

2cm (¾") triangle cutter

Ribbon: light blue

METHOD

Cake Board

1 Knead the pale blue sugarpaste until soft and pliable. Dust the work surface with icing sugar and roll out the sugarpaste to a thickness of 2mm-3mm (less than ⅛"). Cover the cake board, smooth the surface in a circular motion using a cake smoother and trim the excess paste from around the board edge using a knife. Full instructions for covering a cake board are given on page 20. Set the board aside to dry.

Cake

2 To make the parcels, trim the crust from each square cake and one round cake, levelling the top. Cut layers in each cake and then sandwich the layers together using cake filling (see page 18). Stack one square on top of another to make the large parcel. Spread a layer of filling over the surface of each cake as a crumb coat and to help the sugarpaste stick.

3 To make Barney's body, stack the two remaining round cakes one on top of the other and trim the top to taper to a width of 4cm (1½"). Trim around the base to round off the shape, creating a large teardrop

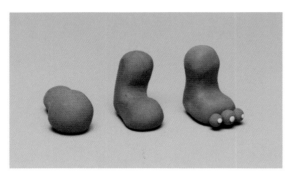

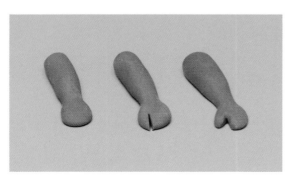

shape. Sandwich the layers with filling and then crumb coat the surface with filling in the same way as before. Set the cakes aside for the surface to firm before covering.

Barney

4 Make Barney's head next to allow for drying time. Roll 200g (7oz) of purple modelling paste into a ball and gently pinch out his oval-shaped muzzle, stroking the surface gently to keep it smooth and dimple-free. Pinch around the mouth area, smoothing back and forth in an upwards curve to create his smile. Stroke either side of his head to narrow it slightly and then make a little dip in the centre by smoothing gently with your fingertips. Push the small end of a ball or bone tool into the eye area to indent sockets. Indent nostrils using the end of a paintbrush.

5 Push a dowelling rod (or lolly stick) into the underside of the head, no more than 2cm (¾") deep. Push the bottom of the dowel into a block of sugarpaste to hold everything in place whilst drying. Make sure that the weight of the head doesn't start to slip down, causing the dowel to protrude from the top of his head.

6 To cover Barney's body, roll out 285g (10oz) of purple sugarpaste and position it over the front and top of his body, smoothing around the shape. Smooth the paste around the back, stretching out any pleats and pinching the join closed. Rub gently to remove the join completely. You may need to add a little edible glue to close stubborn areas if the paste is a little dry. Trim away the excess paste from around the base and smooth gently underneath to round off. (For further instructions, see Covering a Cake with Sugarpaste on pages 18 to 19.)

Parcels

7 Roll out the yellow, orange and pink sugarpaste in turn and cover each square cake, smoothing gently around the shapes, stretching out any pleats and trimming away any excess paste from around the base. Smooth the surface of each with a cake smoother and then position on the covered cake board, leaving room for Barney at the front.

8 Thinly roll out the blue, green and yellow modelling paste in turn and cut circles, squares and triangles. Stick these to the parcels with edible glue. For the bows, first cut strips for the ribbons down the sides of each parcel and secure in place. Cut two

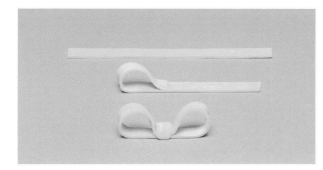

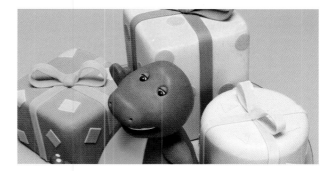

strips for the bow loops, measuring between 10cm and 12cm (4" and 4¾") in length. Loop each one over, secure with a little edible glue and then lay on their sides to harden. When the bow loops are firm, stick in position on top of each parcel with a small, flattened oval for the knot in the centre.

9 To make Barney's tail, roll the remaining purple sugarpaste into a long teardrop shape and flatten the rounded end. Moisten with a little edible glue and then stick in position and smooth the join closed. Position the body on the cake board, leaving room for his legs at the front, and secure in place with a little edible glue.

10 For Barney's green patch at the front, first put aside 5g (just under ¼oz) of green modelling paste and then roll the remainder into a long teardrop shape. Roll out gently with a rolling pin, taking care not to distort the shape. Smooth around the outside edge to round off and then stick in position on Barney's front. Using the remaining green paste, model flattened circles for his spots and then stick in position over his back and tail with edible glue.

11 To make his legs, split 145g (5oz) of purple modelling paste in half. Roll one half into a ball and then roll out from the centre to form his leg. Press down on the full end to flatten, push the excess forward to shape his foot and then pinch to lengthen. Stick in position with edible glue. Repeat for the opposite leg. Indent the bottom of each foot using your fingertip and then stick three purple ball shapes onto the top of each for toes. Finish with tiny flattened balls of yellow modelling paste for toenails.

12 For the arms, first moisten either side of Barney's body with a little edible glue and leave to become tacky. Split 30g (1oz) of purple modelling paste in half. Roll one half into a sausage shape measuring 4cm (1½") in length. Pinch gently at one end to round off the hand, flatten slightly and then make a small cut for the thumb. Round it off gently by smoothing with your fingertips. Make the second arm and stick both in position, holding in place for a few moments until secure.

13 Thinly roll out the black modelling paste and cut a circle using the large circle cutter.

Cut this circle in half and stick one half into Barney's mouth area with the straight edge uppermost. Using white modelling paste, roll two pea-sized balls for his eyes. Thinly roll out the remaining white paste and cut two strips for his teeth, each measuring 5cm (2") in length. Trim each strip so they taper slightly at either end. Moisten Barney's mouth area and stick the mouth in position with both strips curved outwards.

14 Roll a pea-sized ball of purple modelling paste and press down to flatten slightly. Cut this circle in half for the eyelids. Roll two tiny ball shapes of black modelling paste for pupils and thinly roll out and cut two tiny strips for eyelashes. Finish Barney's eyes with a minute dot of white paste to highlight each eye.

15 Remove the dowel from Barney's head and gently push this down into the body, right down to the base, leaving a little protruding to support the head. Moisten the top of Barney's body with a little edible glue and then press the head down over the dowelling until it is in position, tilted up slightly for a fun, happy pose.

16 Trim the board with light blue ribbon.

Mini Barney Cakes

There are two types of mini cakes shown here, both of which are simple to make. The letters and numbers can either be used to decorate the table or given to guests as a sweet treat. I used the first three letters of the alphabet and first three numbers, but you could make the initial letter of all the guests' names, or even spell out their full name if time allows – this would look great as their place name at the party table. They can be flavoured with natural essences or flavourings available from most cake decorating outlets or supermarkets.

Basic instructions for covering mini cakes are given on page 21.

Materials

5cm (2") round and square mini cakes (made using mini pans or cut out from a slab cake)

6cm (2½") triangular cakes (cut out from a slab cake)

Cake filling/crumb coat

Icing (powdered) sugar in a sugar shaker

Sugarpaste (rolled fondant): green; orange; pale blue; pink; purple; yellow

Edible glue (SK)

Equipment

7.5cm (3") round and square cards

Rolling pin

7.5cm (2¾") circle and square cutters (optional)

Sharp knife

Cake smoother

Strong scissors

Letter and number templates (see pages 91 to 92)

METHOD
Parcels

1 To make the parcels, use 5cm (2") round and square mini cakes. Layer and fill the cakes if required and then spread a thin coat of cake filling over the surface to help the sugarpaste stick. Make the fun parcel designs in exactly the same way as the main parcel cakes (see page 68) but using different colour ways.

2 Cover 7.5cm (3") round and square cake cards with matching sugarpaste and place the cakes centrally on the cards, securing in place with a little filling.

Building Blocks

1 Make round and square shapes using a mini pan or a slab cake and cutters. To make the triangle shapes, cut a slab cake into 6cm (2½") strips before cutting into triangles. Spread a thin layer of filling over each cake and cover in your chosen colour of sugarpaste. To accentuate the shape of each block, press down with a cake smoother on each surface area.

2 Place each building block on a cake card and cut the card to size to match the cake perfectly.

Letters and Numbers

Roll thin sausages of sugarpaste and make one letter or number at a time so the paste doesn't dry out before shaping. Using the templates as a guide, follow the contours of the letters and numbers, securing any joins with a little edible glue. Set aside on a flat surface and allow to dry.

Any aspiring ballet dancer would adore this pretty cake. Angelina Ballerina is 'A Little Star With Big Dreams' — here the cute little mouse is leaping through the stars on the way to making her dreams come true.

A Little Star With Big Dreams

Materials

15cm and 25cm (6" and 10") round cakes, 6cm (2½") depth
450g (1lb) cake filling/crumb coat
Icing (powdered) sugar in a sugar shaker
Sugarpaste (rolled fondant):
  1.9kg (4lb 3oz) blue/ mauve
Modelling paste:
  tiny piece of black; tiny piece of green; 800g (1lb 12oz) lilac; tiny piece of pale blue; 30g (1oz) pink; pea-sized piece of red; 45g (1½oz) white
Edible glue (SK)
Sugar stick (see page 15) or piece of dry spaghetti
Dust food colour: pink (SK)
Edible sparkle dust (SK) or edible glitter

Equipment

35cm (14") round cake board (drum)
15cm (6") round cake card
Serrated carving knife
Small, plain-bladed knife
Palette knife
Large and small rolling pins
5 food-grade plastic dowelling rods
Cake smoother
Paintbrushes: flat (for dusting), medium (SK)
A few cocktail sticks
Templates (see pages 92 to 93)
Bone or ball tool
1cm (½") circle cutter
Various small star cutters
Ribbon: lilac

METHOD

Cake Board

1 Knead 450g (1lb) of blue/mauve sugarpaste until soft and pliable, roll out on a sprinkling of icing sugar and cover the cake board. Smooth the surface in a circular motion using a cake smoother, trim neatly around edge using a knife and then set the board aside to dry. Full instructions for covering a cake board are given on page 20.

Cake

2 Trim the crust from each cake and level the top. Cut layers in each and sandwich back together with cake filling (see page 18). Place the large cake centrally on the covered cake board and the smaller cake on the cake card, securing with a dab of cake filling. Spread a thin layer of filling over the surface of both cakes to help the sugarpaste stick. Leave the cakes to firm before covering.

3 Roll out 1kg (2lb 3¼oz) of blue/mauve sugarpaste and cover the large cake (see Covering a Cake with Sugarpaste on pages 18 to 19). Smooth the top surface and around the top edge to remove any trapped air and then smooth the covering down the sides. Trim away any excess

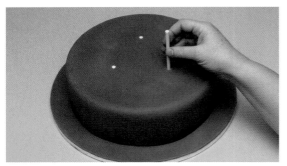

paste, taking care not to mark the cake board. Cover the smaller cake in the same way and set aside.

4 To prevent the weight of the top cake damaging or sinking into the bottom cake, dowel the bottom cake. Push three plastic dowels into the cake, mark each one level with the top surface, remove and then cut to the length of the middle dowel to ensure the cake is level and to prevent any gaps between the two cakes. Re-insert into the cake. Further instructions for dowelling a cake are given on page 20.

Clouds

5 The top cloud needs to be thick at the bottom so that it balances on top of the cake. Give the illusion that it is thinner by rolling a wedge of lilac modelling paste that is thick at one end and thin at the other. Make the graduation smooth so the cloud is also thicker in the centre as again this helps to keep it firm enough to support the figure.

6 Using the template for the top cloud, cut out the shape and smooth around the outside to soften and round off the cut edge. Cut the remaining dowels to 10cm (4") in length and then brush the ends with a little edible glue and push them into the underside of the cloud, leaving most of the length protruding. Place the cloud on a flat surface to dry.

7 Roll out more lilac modelling paste and use the remaining templates to cut out all the clouds for the cake sides. Smooth around the cut edges as before and secure each one in place with a little edible glue.

Angelina Ballerina

8 Build up Angelina Ballerina flat against the top cloud. To make her legs, split 10g (¼oz) of white modelling paste in half. Roll one half into a sausage and stroke the paste at one end to create the pointed toes. Roll gently to indent the ankle and pinch out a heel. Pinch gently halfway along at the front of her leg to mark the knee and then press in behind the knee to bend it gently and give the leg shape. Repeat to make the second leg.

9 To make her ballet slippers, thinly roll out a small piece of pink modelling paste, cut a strip and wrap this around her foot, closing the join at the back. Close the join along the underside of her foot, trim any excess paste away and smooth gently to remove the join completely. Cut tiny strips for the shoe ribbons and secure them in place, crossing them over at the ankles. Stick the legs in position on the cloud.

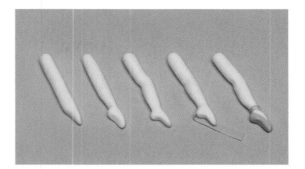

10 To shape her lower body, roll a 5g (just under ¼ oz) ball of pink modelling paste, pinch one side to a point and smooth down. Stick this piece in place with the point joining her legs and smooth the sides down over the top of each leg.

11 For her body, roll 10g (¼ oz) of pink modelling paste into a rounded teardrop. Press down and smooth the sides to straighten. Cut out a semi-circle from the top using a small circle cutter and pinch the paste on either side to lengthen the shoulder straps.

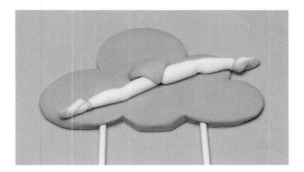

12 Thinly roll out some pink modelling paste to make the tutu. Cut four strips and roll a paintbrush handle over one side to thin and frill the edge. Stick these in position as each one is made, layering them over her lower body.

13 For her neck and chest, roll a piece of white modelling paste the size of two peas together into a ball and then roll the top part between your fingers to create her neck. Smooth the rounded end into the opening of the leotard, keeping the top of her shoulder straps in line with the dip of her neck. Push a sugar stick or piece of dry spaghetti into her neck area, leaving a little protruding ready to support her head.

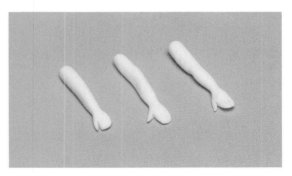

14 Take 5g (just under ¼ oz) of white modelling paste, pinch off one quarter and roll out a thin, tapering tail. Use edible glue to stick in position against the cloud. Split the remainder in half and roll one half into a sausage shape. Narrow towards one end to create a wrist and then round off the hand. Press down on the hand to flatten slightly and stroke to lengthen the fingers. Make a cut on one side no further than halfway in to separate her thumb. Make three further cuts along the top and stroke gently to lengthen her fingers. Roll gently halfway down the arm to create the elbow and then stick in position with a little edible glue. Make the second arm in the same way, cutting the thumb on the opposite side.

15 Roll 10g (¼ oz) of white modelling paste into a rounded teardrop shape for her head and tip up the narrow end slightly. Push a 1cm (½") circle cutter into the underside to indent a semi-circle for her mouth and then add a dimple

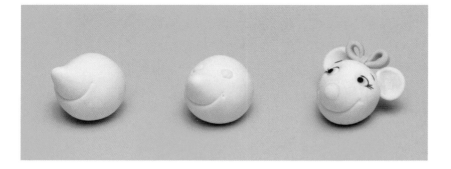

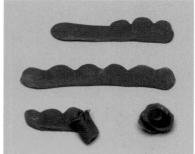

to each corner with a cocktail stick. Indent her eye sockets using the small end of a ball or bone tool.

16 To make her eyes, roll two tiny balls of white modelling paste and stick one into each eye socket, pressing down gently so as not to flatten them completely. Make her irises with tiny balls of pale blue and her pupils with slightly smaller pieces of black. To make her eyelashes and eyebrows, roll minute sausages of black modelling paste between your finger and thumb. Outline the eyes, add three eyelashes on each and a tiny eyebrow just above.

17 Using white modelling paste, roll a tiny ball for the nose and stick in place. Roll two ball shapes for the ears and indent each one with

the large end of a bone or ball tool. For the pink inner ears, roll two tiny balls of pink modelling paste, press down to flatten and stick into each ear with edible glue. Using the bone tool in a circular motion, smooth the pink until it is inlaid into the white surface then glue the ears to the sides of the head.

18 For the bow, roll a small sausage of pink modelling paste to a length of 2.5cm (1"). Press down lengthways with the handle of a paintbrush, turn over and then loop each end, securing in the centre with edible glue. Add a tiny strip for the tie in the centre and then stick in position on Angelina's head.

19 Brush a little pink dust food colour on her cheeks, mouth area and nose. Carefully push the head down onto the sugar stick so that it is tipped up slightly and secure with a little edible glue.

Finishing Touches

20 Thinly roll out the remaining white modelling paste and cut out all the stars using different cutters. Set aside until dry.

21 For Angelina's rose, roll the red modelling paste into a long sausage, press flat and then scallop one side by pressing your finger along the edge repeatedly, gently pulling the paste outwards. Roll up into a spiral and then stroke outwards around the top to turn out the petals. Roll two tiny teardrops from green modelling paste for the leaves and flatten. Stick the rose and leaves onto her tutu with a little edible glue.

22 Stick the stars over the cake and around the clouds with edible glue. Push the top cloud with Angelina Ballerina into position, using a little edible glue to secure at the base.

23 Trim the board with lilac ribbon and sprinkle the cake with edible sparkle dust or edible glitter.

Top Tip

Making the eyelashes and eyebrows can be tricky as the amount of paste is so small, so you may wish to paint them on instead using a very fine paintbrush and black liquid food colour.

Mini Angelina Cakes

With three designs to choose from, making a mixture or multiples of one design would look great on the party table or as little gifts for the party guests. I've kept them simple, with the rose cake being the quickest to make.

Materials

6.5cm (2½") round cakes (made using round mini pans or cut out from a slab cake)
Cake filling/crumb coat
Icing (powdered) sugar in a sugar shaker
Sugarpaste (rolled fondant):
    dark lilac; pink; white
Modelling paste:
    green; red
Edible glue (SK)
Edible sparkle dust (SK)

Equipment

7.5cm (3") round cake cards
Rolling pin
Sharp knife
7cm (2¾") circle cutter (optional)
Ball or bone tool
Cocktail stick
Mini star cutters

Basic instructions for covering mini cakes are given on page 21.

METHOD

Cakes

1 Cover as many round cake cards as required for the mini cakes in the same coloured sugarpaste: I used dark lilac for the ballet slipper design, pink for the rose and white for the stars.

2 When the cakes have cooled, layer and fill each cake if required. To prepare for the covering, spread a thin coat of filling over the surface to help the sugarpaste stick.

3 Cover each cake in your chosen colour of sugarpaste. Roll out the sugarpaste and cover the cake completely, smoothing down and around the shape. To cut around the base quickly and cleanly, place a 7cm (2¾") circle cutter down over the top and cut away any excess paste. Alternatively, trim around the base with a knife. Use a cake smoother to achieve a neat, smooth surface. Place each covered cake on a covered cake card.

Ballet Slippers

1 To make a ballet slipper, roll 5g (just under ¼oz) of pink modelling paste into a fat sausage shape. Push a ball or bone tool into the front, smoothing the paste over the tool slightly. Move the ball or bone tool back and forth inside the slipper and round off the heel by moving the tool in a circular motion.

2 Pinch gently halfway along on either side to shape the slipper and then stick in position. Add little strips of pink for ribbons. Repeat for the second slipper, turning it on its side. Use stars to decorate around the sides.

Rose

1 Roll a small ball of red modelling paste into a long sausage measuring 6cm-7cm (2½"-2¾") in length. Press or roll flat and then pull out a scalloped edge using your fingertip. Turn the paste over and then roll up into a spiral. Gently bend over the petals at the top and then pinch underneath the rose so the centre pops out a little, giving a rounded shape to the flower.

2 Roll tiny teardrops of green modelling paste for leaves and indent down the centre of each using a cocktail stick. Sprinkle the top of the cake with edible sparkle dust or edible glitter flakes.

Stars

Mark star shapes into the surface of the soft cake covering using various star cutters. Cut out stars using dark and light pink and lilac modelling paste. To build up the centre, gently push some larger stars into the covering and then stick other stars onto it, building some up higher.

The fun and heroic adventures of Fireman Sam continue to delight and inspire young children. Sam standing proudly next to Jupiter, his fire engine, makes a fun and appealing cake that's sure to be popular.

Materials

25cm (10") square cake, 5cm (2") depth

450g (1lb) cake filling/crumb coat

Icing (powdered) sugar in a sugar shaker

Sugarpaste (rolled fondant):
  90g (3oz) black; 450g (1lb) dark blue; 90g (3oz) pale grey; 800g (1lb 12oz) red

Modelling paste:
  22g (¾oz) black; 5g (just under ¼oz) chestnut brown; 35g (1¼oz) dark blue; 90g (3oz) dark grey; 22g (¾oz) flesh; 90g (3oz) pale grey; tiny piece of pale blue; 15g (½oz) red; 20g (¾oz) white; 90g (3oz) yellow

Edible glue (SK)

Sugar stick (see page 15) or dry spaghetti

Liquid food colours: black, white (SK)

Edible metallic paint: silver (SK)

Edible paint: white (SK)

Dust food colour: red (SK)

Equipment

35cm (14") round cake board (drum)

Serrated carving knife

Small, plain-bladed knife

Palette knife

Large and small rolling pins

Cake smoother

Paintbrushes: fine, medium (SK)

A few cocktail sticks

Piping nozzle (tip): no. 3

Ruler

Bone or ball tool

Sheet of card

Templates (see page 93)

Miniature circle cutter or large plastic drinking straw

4cm (1½") square cutter

2cm (¾") circle cutter

Ribbon: dark blue

METHOD

Cake Board

1 Knead the dark blue sugarpaste until soft and pliable, roll out on a work surface lightly sprinkled with icing sugar and cover the cake board. Smooth the surface in a circular motion using a cake smoother. Trim the excess paste from around the board edge using a knife and then set the board aside to dry. Full instructions for covering a cake board are given on page 20.

Cake

2 Trim the crust from the cake and level the top. Cut the cake exactly in half. Cut layers in each cake and then position one on top of the other. To shape the windscreen, cut in from the top 1.5cm (½"), slicing diagonally downwards and outwards to the centre layer. To shape the top, measure 10cm (4") from the front and make a 1.5cm (½") deep cut. Slice from this cut to the back of the engine and remove the spare piece of cake.

3 Sandwich all the layers together with filling and assemble on the centre of the cake board with a little filling underneath, and then spread a layer over the surface of the cake as a crumb coat and to

help the sugarpaste stick. Leave the buttercream to firm before covering. (For further instructions, see Preparing a Sponge Cake on page 18.)

FIREMAN SAM

Boots and Trousers

4 To make his boots, split 5g (just under ¼oz) of black modelling paste in half, roll into teardrop shapes, press down on the narrow end of each to round off, and then set aside.

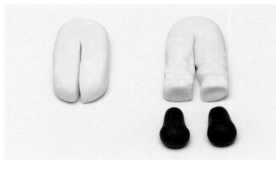

5 For his trousers, roll 22g (¾oz) of yellow modelling paste into a sausage shape measuring 3.5cm (1¼") in length and press down to flatten slightly. Make a cut along three-quarters of the length to separate the legs and then round off the edges at the front and back of each. To help lengthen the legs and also create the wrinkles, roll a paintbrush handle into the surface of each leg to create uneven rings, smoothing gently with your fingertip if they become too deep or angular. Cut the bottom of each trouser leg straight and then stick the shoes in place. Lay flat until firm and then stand upright to dry.

Tunic

6 To make his tunic, roll 22g (¾oz) of dark blue modelling paste into a sausage shape measuring 3.5cm (1¼") in length and press down to flatten slightly. So the tunic sits over the top of the trousers, gently indent the bottom and pinch out the paste all the way around the edge. Make a small indentation at the back for the kick pleat. Lay the tunic flat and indent the join at the front using a knife. Position the tunic onto the trousers and use a little edible glue to secure.

Belt

7 To make his belt, thinly roll out a small piece of black modelling paste and cut a thin strip. Stick in position around the tunic with the join at the front (this will be hidden by the buckle later). To make the axe, roll a pea-sized amount of yellow modelling paste into a sausage shape and stick in position for the axe handle. For the top, first split 5g (just under ¼oz) of red

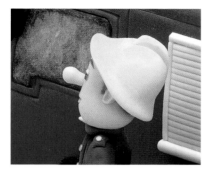

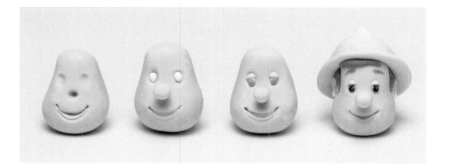

modelling paste in half and set aside one piece for the torch later. Roll the second piece into a teardrop shape and press down on the full end to flatten. Cut this end straight for the blade and then stick in position on top of the handle and against the tunic.

8 To make the torch, roll the remaining half into a sausage shape and round off one end. Press down on the rounded end to flatten and then stick in position against the belt and tunic. Stick tiny strips of black over the handle of the torch and axe for the supports. Make two tiny square pouches for either side of the belt, indent flaps on each using the tip of a knife and stick in position.

9 Using 10g (¼oz) of dark blue modelling paste, roll one quarter into a ball, press down to flatten slightly and stick in position for his tunic collar. For sleeves, first moisten either side of the tunic with edible glue and leave to become tacky. Split the remaining piece in half and roll into sausage shapes measuring 4cm (1½") in length. So the hands are held securely, hollow out the end of each by pushing in the handle of a paintbrush and roll around

a little to open up the sleeve. Stick each sleeve into position, smoothing gently but firmly into the shoulder area until secure. Push the sugar stick or dry spaghetti down into the figure, leaving it protruding at the top to help hold the head in place later.

10 Thinly roll out a pea-sized amount of dark blue modelling paste and cut two tiny strips for the tunic shoulder flaps. Roll out some pale grey modelling paste and cut twelve circles for buttons using the no. 3 plain piping nozzle. Sticking two onto the back flap, two on each shoulder and the remainder down the front of the tunic. For the buckle, roll out a small piece and make a hole in the centre using the end of a paintbrush, squaring it off a little. Cut around this hole and stick in position. Paint the buttons, buckle, axe blade and torch light with edible silver paint.

Head

11 To make his head, roll 15g (½oz) of flesh modelling paste into a ball and then roll gently to narrow the top slightly. Cut away the back of his head at a slant down to halfway ready for the hat later.

Push a cocktail stick into the bottom and use as a support whilst working on the head. Indent his smile using the miniature circle cutter or a drinking straw pushed in at an upwards angle. To make the protruding bottom lip, push in once again, just underneath, and then dimple the corners of his mouth using a cocktail stick.

12 For his nose, first indent a small hole just above his smile using the end of a paintbrush. Roll a teardrop using a pea-sized amount of flesh modelling paste and stick the point into the hole, pressing the end up to create a rounded, turned-up nose.

13 Indent two small eye sockets using the end of a paintbrush and roll two tiny balls of white modelling paste for the eyes, sticking in position with a tiny touch of edible glue. Stick two tiny flattened circles of pale blue paste onto the centre

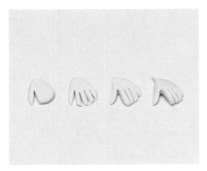

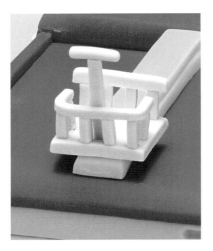

for his irises and then two slightly smaller circles of black for his pupils.

14 To make the eyelids, roll a tiny oval shape of flesh modelling paste, press flat, cut in half and stick in position with the rounded edge of each at the top. For eyelashes, roll a minute amount of black between your finger and thumb until very fine, cut two small pieces and use to edge the bottom of each eyelid. If you'd prefer to paint them on instead, use a very fine paintbrush with only a little liquid food colour so it doesn't flood and make the lines heavy. Paint a tiny highlight of white onto each using edible white paint. Brush a tiny amount of red dust colour onto his bottom lip.

15 Remove the cocktail stick and gently push the head down onto the sugar stick or dry spaghetti, securing at the neck with a little edible glue.

Hands

16 To make the hands, first moisten the end of each sleeve with edible glue and leave to become tacky. Using large pea-sized amounts of flesh modelling paste for each, roll one into a teardrop shape and press down to flatten slightly. From the rounded end, cut the thumb on one side down to halfway, keeping the cut straight. Make three shorter cuts along the top to separate the fingers. Pull the thumb down and press on the point to round off. Gently roll each finger

to lengthen, push together and then stroke around to naturally curve the hand. Smooth the thumb down towards the palm. Pinch to shape the wrist and narrow into a point so it will slot into the end of the sleeve easily. Repeat for the second hand, cutting the thumb on the opposite side.

Hat

17 Roll 10g (¼oz) of yellow modelling paste into a ball and then indent the centre, making a dip that will fit onto the top of Fireman Sam's head. For the brim, pinch gently around the rim so it turns up gently, making it a little deeper at the back. Stick in position and add a tapered strip at the front.

Hair

18 To make the hair, roll different sized teardrop shapes with chestnut brown modelling paste and stick in position around the underside of his hat, making a long one for the quiff at the front. Roll two minute tapered sausage shapes for the eyebrows. Set the complete figure aside to dry.

Cage

19 Roll out some pale grey modelling paste to a depth of 0.5cm (just under ¼") and cut a square for the base of the cage using the 4cm (1½") square cutter. Cut ten 1cm (½") strips for the spindles and stick these evenly around the edge of the square. To complete

the cage, cut a long strip for the pole handle measuring 4cm (1½") in length and roll a small handle for the top. Cut two further strips to edge the top of the spindles. Assemble the cage except for the pole handle to allow for drying time and then set aside.

Fire Engine

20 Thinly roll out some black sugarpaste and cut a strip 4cm (1½") deep to fit around the base of the fire engine. Glue in place and smooth the join closed at the back. Roll out the pale grey sugarpaste and cover the back of the engine only, leaving a 1.5cm (½") gap from the bottom. Using a ruler or straight edge, mark the horizontal and vertical lines and then indent a handle into the top right hand corner using the end of a paintbrush.

21 Roll out 115g (4oz) of red sugarpaste and cut a piece to cover the top of the fire engine on the back half only. Smooth the end down over the grey covering at the rear of the engine; if the line distorts, trim to a straight line using a ruler.

22 Make the front and side window templates from card and set aside. To cover the sides of the engine, roll out 500g (1lb 1¾oz) of red sugarpaste and cut pieces to cover each side, keeping the end and top edge larger and rounding off the top corner. Cut out spaces for the wheels, the front two measuring 5cm (2") at the widest point along the bottom and 8cm (3") for the two back wheels. Using the back of a knife, mark two vertical lines separating compartments using the side window template as a guide. For the side windows, press the side window template gently into the surface of the sugarpaste; this will slightly indent the window. Mark the lined edging with a knife. Reverse the piece of card and repeat on the opposite side.

23 Roll out 90g (3oz) of red sugarpaste and cut a piece to cover the front of the engine. Indent the front window using the card template and mark the edge as before. Using the red trimmings cut a strip for the front of the engine measuring 11cm × 2cm (4½" × ¾") and round off the top two corners. Stick in position with a little edible glue. Roll a thin sausage for underneath and smooth down the opposite ends. Thinly roll out and cut a further strip to hold the lights and grille.

24 To cover the top of the engine, roll out the remaining red sugarpaste and cut a piece to fit. Place in position and smooth the top edge gently to round it off.

Use a cake smoother to achieve a completely smooth surface.

25 Thinly roll out the grey modelling paste and cut shapes for the shutter doors, two measuring 2.5cm x 4cm (1" x 1½"), two 5cm x 4cm (2" x 1½") and two 2.5cm x 5cm (1" x 2"). Indent fine, even lines with a ruler. Cut strips to edge the side of each, roll a sausage to go along the bottom and then set aside to dry on a flat surface before positioning. Model two tiny teardrop-shaped door handles. Make two headlights and mark a faint criss-cross pattern with a knife. Make two flattened circles for the top of the engine and shape two horns by rolling sausages of grey modelling paste, rounding off each end with one larger than the other and then indenting the large end with a ball or bone tool.

26 Roll a 15g (½oz) sausage of white modelling paste for the engine's front bumper and stick in position along the bottom, keeping a gap between the bumper and the cake board surface. Thinly roll out some red modelling paste and cut strips for the bumper with a triangle shape in the centre. Roll two tiny balls for the back lights.

27 To make the grille, thinly roll out some grey modelling paste, indent a folded piece of card into the surface and then cut around the indentations. Stick this in position between the headlights. Using the remaining dark blue paste, model the emergency lights for the top, front and back of the engine.

28 Thickly roll out the remaining yellow modelling paste and cut strips for the top of the engine. Make the top one shorter, leaving room for the cage, and cut it slightly narrower. Stick the cage and handle in position, ensuring it is well balanced.

29 Thinly roll out the remaining black modelling paste and cut strips to edge around each wheel arch. To make the wheels, split the dark grey modelling paste into six pieces, roll into ball shapes and indent the centre using the 2cm (¾")

circle cutter. To make the wheel hubs, roll out the remaining white and red modelling paste and cut three circles of each colour. Cut each circle into quarters and then assemble these into the wheel centres, finishing each wheel with a small ball of red.

30 Dilute a little black liquid food colour with a little cooled, boiled water until slightly translucent. Paint a 'wash' over each window, followed by a little edible silver paint. Paint silver onto Fireman Sam's buttons, buckle, along the edge of his axe and on top of his torch for the torch light.

31 To finish, trim the board with dark blue ribbon.

Mini Fireman Sam Cakes

Materials

6.5cm (2½") cakes dariol (cup-shaped) cakes (made using a dariol mould, a large muffin tin or a silicone mould)

6.5cm (2½") round cakes (made using round mini pans or cut out from a slab cake)

Cake filling/crumb coat

Icing (powdered) sugar in a sugar shaker

Sugarpaste (rolled fondant):
  pale blue; red; white; yellow

Modelling paste:
  golden brown; grey; red

Liquid food colours: black, red, yellow (SK)

Equipment

7.5cm (3") round cake cards
10cm (4") oval cake cards
Rolling pin
Sharp knife
Set of 3 circle cutters, the largest 6cm (2¼")
Cake smoother
Paintbrushes: fine, medium (SK)

Basic instructions for covering mini cakes are given on page 21.

These four fun designs are quite straightforward to make, although some a little more time consuming than others. Fireman Sam's helmet is quickest to make whereas the fire bucket with the handle will take a little more time. You could make a mixture of them all, or create a display of one design for the table.

METHOD

Fire Bucket

1 Layer and fill the dariol-shaped cakes if required then spread a thin layer of filling over the surface to crumb coat the cakes. Place on 7.5cm (3") round cake cards covered with white sugarpaste.

2 Cover the top of the cakes first with a 6cm (2¼") circle of pale blue sugarpaste. Use the underside of two smaller circle cutters to indent the ripples on the surface, smoothing the lines gently with your fingertips. Indenting the paste also makes the circle slightly larger so it fits perfectly on the top of the cake.

3 To cover the sides, roll out some red sugarpaste and cut a strip measuring 20cm (8") in length and 1.5cm (½") deeper than the height of the cake. Carefully roll up the strip and then wrap it around the cake, securing the join closed with a little edible glue. You may need to trim some excess away to achieve a neat join. Indent rings around the bucket using the handle of a paintbrush.

4 For the bucket handle, roll 10g (¼oz) of grey modelling paste into a sausage measuring 16cm (6¼") long, round off each end and press down to flatten slightly. Leave to harden before positioning. Brush edible glue on either side of the bucket and allow it to become tacky before sticking the handle in place. Add small, flattened circles of red for the bolts. Leave the cake to dry completely before painting the wording.

5 Use black liquid food colour and a fine paintbrush to paint 'FIRE' onto the side of the bucket. Allow to dry.

Hose

1 Cover a 7.5cm (3") round cake card with white sugarpaste for each cake. Layer and fill 6.5cm (2½") round cakes if required then apply the crumb coat. Cover the cakes with white sugarpaste, trim neatly at the base and use a cake smoother to achieve a smooth surface. Place in the centre of the covered cake cards.

2 For the hose, roll 30g (1oz) of red modelling paste into a long sausage shape and spiral it around the base of the cake, lifting the end up to the top. For the hose end, roll 5g (just under ¼oz) of golden brown modelling paste into a long teardrop shape and roll a knife over the surface to indent different-sized rings. Finish with a little pale blue modelling paste to make water droplets and spills.

Helmet

1 To make the helmet shape, turn a 6.5cm (2½") dariol cake or cupcake upside down and place slightly off-centre on a 10cm (4") oval cake card (the rim should be slightly fuller at the back). Round off the cake if necessary and apply a crumb coat.

2 To make the piece at the top, roll a tapering sausage of yellow sugarpaste, cut the full end straight and stick on top of the cake.

3 Cover the whole cake and board with yellow sugarpaste. Run your finger around the shape at the top to give it more definition and smooth around the base to indent the paste slightly. Trim neatly around the edge of the cake card.

Top Tip

If you have any slight imperfections in the covering, you can always add tiny teardrops of light blue paste to resemble splashes of water.

Fire

1 This fun design was baked in a 6.5cm (2½") round mini pan. Trim off the top and bottom edges to round off slightly before applying a crumb coat. Cover a 7.5cm (3") round cake card with yellow sugarpaste and place the cake in the centre.

2 For the flames, model different-sized teardrop shapes from yellow sugarpaste. Make a large one for the top of the cake and then build up the flames around it until the cake is covered down to the base.

3 Dilute a little orange and red liquid food colouring with some cooled, boiled water and paint streaks of each colour over the surface.

Top Tip

This design is easy to decorate, so you could turn it into a fun activity at a children's party.

Templates

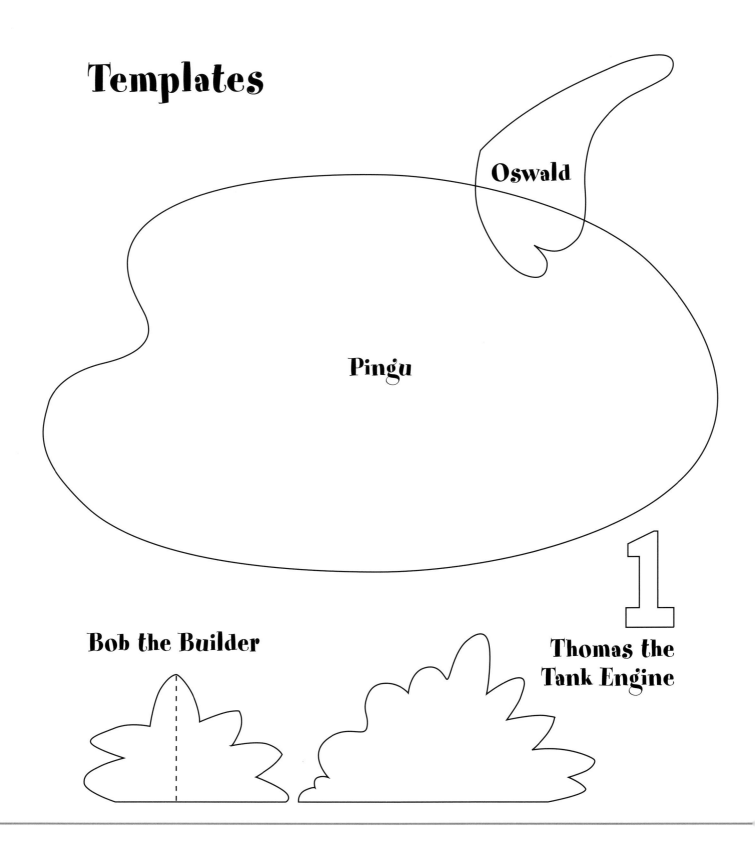

Oswald

Pingu

Bob the Builder

1

Thomas the
Tank Engine

Rainbow Magic

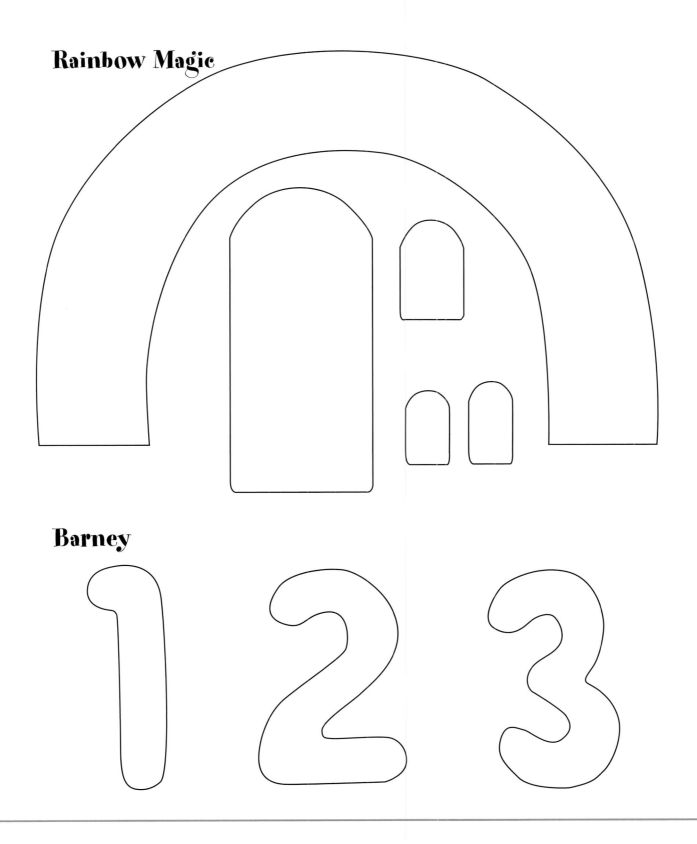

Barney

Barney

Angelina Ballerina

Angelina Ballerina

Fireman Sam

Suppliers

Shops

UK

Jane Asher Party Cakes
24 Cale Street
London
SW3 3QU
Tel: 020 7584 6177
Fax: 020 7584 6179
E-mail: info@janeasher.com
Website: www.jane-asher.co.uk

Pipedreams
2 Bell Lane
Eton Wick
Windsor
Berkshire
SL4 6JP
Tel/Fax: 01753 865682
E-mail: pipedreaming@btinternet.com
Website: www.pipedreams-sugarcraft.co.uk

Squires Kitchen Sugarcraft (SK)
Squires House
3 Waverley Lane
Farnham
Surrey
GU9 8BB
Tel: 0845 22 55 67 1/2 (from UK)
+44 (0)1252 711749 (from overseas)
E-mail: customer@squires-shop.com
Websites: www.squires-shop.com
www.squiresschool.co.uk

Sugar Celebrations
37 Faringdon Road
Swindon
Wiltshire
SN1 5AR
Tel: 01793 513549
and
80 Westgate Street
Gloucester
GL1 2NZ
Tel: 01452 308848
E-mail: girls@sugarcelebrations.com
Website: www.sugarcelebrations.com

Australia

Cakedeco
Shop 7
Port Phillip Arcade
228 Flinders Street
Melbourne
Australia
T: +61 (0) 3 9654 5335
cakedeco@optusnet.com.au

Iced Affair
53 Church St.
Camperdown
NSW 2050
Australia
T: +61 (0) 2 9519 3679
icedaffair@iprimus.com.au
Website: www.icedaffair.com.au

Susie Q Cake Decorating Centre
Shop 4
372 Keilor Road
Niddrie
Victoria 3042
Australia
Tel: +61 (0) 3 9379 2275
Website: www.susie-qcake.com.au

The Netherlands

Planet Cake®
Zuidplein 117
3083 CN
Rotterdam
The Netherlands
Tel: +31 (0)10 290 91 30
E-mail: info@cake.nl
Website: www.cake.nl

Sweden

Tårtdecor
Bultgatan 14
442 40 KUNGÄLV
Svierge
Tel: +46 303 514 70
E-mail: info@tartdecor.se
Website: www.tartdecor.se

Manufacturers and Distributors

UK

Ceefor Cakes
PO Box 443
Leighton Buzzard
Bedfordshire
LU7 1AJ
Tel: 01525 375237
Fax: 01525 385414
E-mail: info@ceeforcakes.co.uk
Website: www.ceeforcakes.co.uk

Confectionery Supplies
Unit 11a, b and c
Foley Trading Estate
Hereford
HR1 2SF
Tel: 01432 371451
029 2037 2161 (mail order)
E-mail: kclements@btinternet.com
Website: www.confectionerysupplies.co.uk

Design Acrylics
28 The Green
Mountsorrel
Leicester
LE12 7AF
E-mail: designacrylics@gmail.com

Guy, Paul & Co. Ltd.
Unit 10, The Business Centre
Corinium Industrial Estate
Raans Road
Amersham
Buckinghamshire
HP6 6FB
Tel: 01494 432121
E-mail: sales@guypaul.co.uk
Website: www.guypaul.co.uk

Renshaw
Crown Street
Liverpool
L8 7RF
E-mail: enquiries@renshaw-nbf.co.uk
Website: www.renshaw-nbf.co.uk
Manufacturers of Regalice and marzipan.

Squires Group
Squires House
3 Waverley Lane
Farnham
Surrey
GU9 8BB
Tel: 0845 22 55 67 1/2 (from UK)
+44 (0)1252 711749 (from overseas)
E-mail: info@squires-group.co.uk
Websites: www.squires-group.co.uk
www.cakesandsugarcraft.co.uk
www.squires-exhibition.co.uk

USA

Beryl's Cake Decorating & Pastry Supplies
PO Box 1584
N. Springfield, VA
USA
Tel: +1 800 488 2749
Website: www.beryls.com

Caljava International School of Cake Decorating and Sugar Craft
19519 Business Center Drive
Northridge, CA 91324
USA
Tel: +1 818 718 2707
Fax: +1 818 718 2715
E-mail: caljava@aol.com
Website: www.cakevisions.com

Global Sugar Art, LLC
28 Plattsburgh Plaza
Plattsburgh, NY 12901
USA
Tel: +1-800-420-6088
E-mail: sales@globalsugarart.com
Website: www.globalsugarart.com

Guilds

The British Sugarcraft Guild
Wellington House
Messeter Place
London
SE9 5DP
Tel: 020 8859 6943
Website: www.bsguk.org

About the Author

Debbie Brown is an accomplished cake decorator, author and sugarcraft tutor, with many titles published on novelty cake decoration. She is the UK's best-selling author of novelty cake books and is renowned all over the world for her work.

When she is not travelling extensively to teach her craft, Debbie works from her studio near London, UK, producing cake designs for books, magazine projects, consultancy and for private commissions.

For information on tuition, see www.debbiebrownscakes.co.uk or e-mail debra.brown@btinternet.com. To find out more about Debbie's courses at Squires Kitchen's International School of Cake Decorating and Sugarcraft, visit www.squiresschool. co.uk or call the Course Co-ordinator on 0845 22 55 67 1/2 (+44 1252 711749 from outside the UK).